ALSO BY MARGE PIERCY

POETRY

The Crooked Inheritance

Colors Passing Through Us

The Art of Blessing the Day

Early Grrrl

What Are Big Girls Made Of?

Mars and Her Children

Available Light

My Mother's Body

Stone, Paper, Knife

Circles on the Water (Selected Poems)

The Moon Is Always Female

The Twelve-Spoked Wheel Flashing

Living in the Open

To Be of Use

4-Telling (with Bob Hershon, Emmett
    Jarrett, and Dick Lourie)

Hard Loving

Breaking Camp

NOVELS

Sex Wars

The Third Child

Three Women

Storm Tide (with Ira Wood)

City of Darkness, City of Light

The Longings of Women

He, She and It

Summer People

Gone to Soldiers

Fly Away Home

Braided Lives

Vida

The High Cost of Living

Woman on the Edge of Time

Small Changes

Dance the Eagle to Sleep

Going Down Fast

OTHER

Pesach for the Rest of Us

So You Want to Write: How to Master
    the Craft of Writing Fiction and the
    Personal Narrative (with Ira Wood),
    1st & 2nd editions

The Last White Class (Play) (with Ira
    Wood)

Sleeping with Cats: A Memoir

Parti-Colored Blocks for a Quilt
    (Essays)

Early Ripening: American Women's
    Poetry Now (Anthology)

THE HUNGER MOON

The Hunger Moon

NEW AND SELECTED POEMS

1980–2010

Marge Piercy

Alfred A. Knopf · New York · 2011

THIS IS A BORZOI BOOK
PUBLISHED BY ALFRED A. KNOPF

Knopf, Borzoi Books, and the colophon are
registered trademarks of Random House, Inc.

Most of the poems in this collection originally appeared in the following works:
Stone, Paper, Knife, copyright © 1983 by Marge Piercy (Alfred A. Knopf)
My Mother's Body, copyright © 1985 by Marge Piercy (Alfred A. Knopf)
Available Light, copyright © 1988 by Middlemarsh, Inc. (Alfred A. Knopf)
Mars and Her Children, copyright © 1992 by Middlemarsh, Inc. (Alfred A. Knopf)
What Are Big Girls Made Of?, copyright © 1997 by Middlemarsh, Inc. (Alfred A. Knopf)
Early Grrrl, copyright © 1999 by Middlemarsh, Inc. (The Leapfrog Press)
The Art of Blessing the Day, copyright © 1999 by Middlemarsh, Inc. (Alfred A. Knopf)
Colors Passing Through Us, copyright © 2003 by Middlemarsh, Inc. (Alfred A. Knopf)
The Crooked Inheritance, copyright © 2006 by Middlemarsh, Inc. (Alfred A. Knopf)

Some new poems in this collection were previously published in the following
periodicals: *Blue Fifth, Fifth Wednesday, 5 AM, Basalt, Poesis, The Arava Review,
Rattle, Tryst, Midstream, Jewish Women's Literary Annual, Ibbetson Street Magazine,*
and *Contemporary World Literature.*

Library of Congress Cataloguing-in-Publication Data
Piercy, Marge.
The hunger moon : new and selected poems, 1980–2010 / by Marge Piercy.—1st ed.
p. cm.
ISBN 978-0-307-59410-5
I. Title.
PS3566.I4H86 2011
811'.54—dc22 2010030987

Jacket photograph by Oliver Wasow/Gallery Stock
Jacket design by Abby Weintraub

Manufactured in the United States of America
First Edition

For Ira aka Woody because of his love,
his help and his willingness to put his shoulder to the great wheel

CONTENTS

from AVAILABLE LIGHT

from MARS AND HER CHILDREN

from WHAT ARE BIG GIRLS MADE OF?

from EARLY GRRRL

from THE ART OF BLESSING THE DAY

from COLORS PASSING THROUGH US

from THE CROOKED INHERITANCE

Some NEW POEMS

INTRODUCTION

What's the difference between the poetry in *Circles on the Water,*
which summarized my first seven books, and this volume, which
pulls some poems from the last nine? A lot has changed in almost
thirty years. In 1982, I had already moved to Cape Cod and the natu-
ral world had begun to provide me with new, rich sources of imagery
and experience. I am still politically engaged, as a feminist, as one
concerned with environmental issues, with problems of health and
aging, with equality and rights for all, with economic oppression,
with various local issues—although perhaps a little more relaxed
about politics in my social life. Nonetheless, my anger against those
who consider themselves entitled to rights that they would deny to
others has not diminished and I doubt ever will. Nor does my rage
against those who use power to belittle, injure, or kill others whom
they consider inferior to themselves.

In 1981, the first night of Hanukkah, my mother died, and for the
next year I said Kaddish for her daily, as I do every year on her yahr-
zeit. I was saying gibberish because I had never been bat mitzvahed
and knew no Hebrew. Needing to understand what I was saying for
my mother, I began to learn at least enough to read and comprehend
prayers. This began my reemergence into Judaism. I had begun to
host seders for Pesach after the divorce from my second husband and
to study the origins, history, and meaning of Pesach. Shortly after-
ward I entered into the never-ending process of writing my own hag-
gadah, one poem, one passage at a time. [It's still ongoing, for in spite
of my writing *Pesach for the Rest of Us,* it will never be finished.] I was
one of the founders of a havurah Am haYam, people of the sea, on the
Outer Cape, a Jewish lay group, and one of the people who ran it for
ten years. All of that brought new elements into my poetry. Through
Kabbalah, I began to meditate. It keeps me from imploding.

The death of my mother dug a hole in my life and I have written about her suffering and hard life ever since. In some ways, hers is the face of the women I have fought for and written about. She is a frequent presence in my imagination and my memory. I have also returned frequently to my warm memories of my grandmother Hannah, who gave me my religious education and unconditional love. As I age, I have become aware of how much they gave me.

I married Ira Wood in 1982 after being in a relationship with him since 1976. While I had written considerable love poetry before, it was mostly poems of unhappy love, rocky affairs, longings unsatisfied. I began to write poems of fulfilled love and about the ongoing joys and problems of living monogamously through the years. I don't believe I had ever before been happy in any intimate relationship for longer than a matter of days or weeks. I have never regretted my many experiences and adventures when I was in an open relationship, but it is certainly simpler and less demanding to be monogamous on those rare occasions when it actually works out. For us, it has. I think we are each other's *bashert*. I cannot imagine being truly mated with anyone else over time. We still prefer talking with each other to anybody else.

As I grow older, I have had trouble with my eyes—cataracts and glaucoma and extreme myopia inherited from my parents—and my knees. I explore what aging means to me, how it actually happens to me. I have experienced the death of not only my parents and my brother but many friends. My own death has become far more real to me. That also has influenced my poetry. Death is not a sometime visitor but a kind of shadow.

Everything I learn and experience enriches my poetry, whatever its source.

I am an intellectually curious person. I do a great deal of research for my novels and my nonfiction works. Out of every epoch of history I study, out of every life and career I explore, poems issue—not from the narrative itself but from what I observe and learn. Whether it's the French Revolution, appeals court, roses, herring, the origins of dates and almonds, my storehouse of imagery grows wider and deeper.

I first learned how American I am when I lived in France with my first husband. Since then I have continued to explore what this means, when I am so often at odds with the choices my government makes in this country and in the world outside of us. So often we are dangerous and destructive, and this consciousness is something that also informs my poetry.

I have explored my own childhood and adolescence far more as I age than I did when I was younger. In all of my last nine books, there are poems that deal with my formative years in Detroit, in my family, in the hood, among the friends and enemies I had then. Writing my memoir, *Sleeping with Cats,* forced me to return to many eras in my life that I had not entered in decades. It made my life far more vivid to me.

Ira, cats and the garden and local wildlife and the ocean and the seasons and the weather are part of the daily web of my life. As I write this, we have been snowed in for two days and cannot get out of our driveway. Hurricanes, nor'easters, ice storms, thunder and lightning, prolonged drought are events that impact us powerfully. My life is very different from that of most poets now because I do not have an affiliation with any college or university. I live as I can off my writing and gigs—readings, workshops, speeches, contests I judge, mini-residencies. I live in a village up close with nature in benign and hostile forms—my imposition of value on what simply is and what we have through our greed and carelessness caused. I live not with academics and writers as friends, although I have some of each, but in a locality where my friends are oystermen, a retired homicide detective, a retired OR nurse, carpenters, artists, a librarian, actors, a bank manager, a lawyer, a boat captain, a plumber. Ira Wood has been a selectman, one of the five people who run the town, for a number of years. That also brings us into contact with a wide range of people, both local and summer people. All of this feeds into my poetry, and I believe it's one of the reasons so many people can relate to what I write, as I hope you can. My poems read well aloud. I like to perform them. So do others. Naturally, I think I do it best.

My poems go out into the world as best they can in print or on the Internet and get used for memorial services, love notes, political organizing, teaching, religious services, weddings, and bar and bat mitzvot. All that is appropriate. I write the poems, but they belong to whoever wants them. That's how poetry stays alive—in the minds and voices of those who want to share it. I hear regularly from people for whom my poetry is meaningful and part of their consciousness. That means a great deal to me.

from
Stone, Paper, Knife

A key to common lethal fungi

What rots it is taking
for granted. To assume what
is given you is laid on like the water
that rushes from the faucet singing
when you turn the tap. Wait
till the reservoir goes dry
to learn how precious are those
clear diamond drops.

We hunt our lovers like deer
through the thorny thickets and after
we have caught love we start
eating it to the bone.
We use it up in hamburgers
complaining of monotony.
We walk all over the common miracles
without bothering to wipe our feet.
Then we wonder why we need more
and more salt to taste our food.

My old man, my old lady, my
ball and chain: listen, even the cat
you found starving in the alley
who purrs you to sleep dancing
with kneading paws in your hair
will vanish if your heart closes its fist.

Habit's fine dust chokes us.
As in a city the streetlights
and neon signs prevent us from viewing
the stars, so the casual noise, the smoke
of ego turning over its engine blinds
us till we can no longer see past
our minor needs to the major constellations
of the ram, the hunter, the swan
that guide our finite gaze
through the infinite dark.

The common living dirt

The small ears prick on the bushes,
furry buds, shoots tender and pale.
The swamp maples blow scarlet.
Color teases the corner of the eye,
delicate gold, chartreuse, crimson,
mauve speckled, just dashed on.

The soil stretches naked. All winter
hidden under the down comforter of snow,
delicious now, rich in the hand
as chocolate cake: the fragrant busy
soil the worm passes through her gut
and the beetle swims in like a lake.

As I kneel to place the seeds
careful as stitching, I am in love.
You are the bed we all sleep on.
You are the food we eat, the food
we ate, the food we will become.
We are walking trees rooted in you.

You can live thousands of years
undressing in the spring your black
body, your red body, your brown body
penetrated by the rain. Here
is the goddess unveiled,
the earth opening her strong thighs.

Yet you grow exhausted with bearing
too much, too soon, too often, just
as a woman wears through like an old rug.
We have contempt for what we spring
from. Dirt, we say, you're dirt
if we were not all your children.

We have lost the simplest gratitude.
We lack the knowledge we showed ten
thousand years past, that you live

a goddess but mortal, that what we take
must be returned; that the poison we drop
in you will stunt our children's growth.

Tending a plot of your flesh binds
me as nothing ever could, to the seasons,
to the will of the plants, clamorous
in their green tenderness. What
calls louder than the cry of a field
of corn ready, or trees of ripe peaches?

I worship on my knees, laying
seeds in you, that worship rooted
in need, in hunger, in kinship,
flesh of the planet with my own flesh,
a ritual of compost, a litany of manure.
My garden's a chapel, but a meadow

gone wild in grass and flower
is a cathedral. How you seethe
with little quick ones, vole, field
mouse, shrew and mole in their thousands,
rabbit and woodchuck. In you rest
the jewels of the genes wrapped in seed.

Power warps because it involves joy
in domination; also because it means
forgetting how we too starve, break
like a corn stalk in the wind, how we
die like the spinach of drought,
how what slays the vole slays us.

Because you can die of overwork, because
you can die of the fire that melts
rock, because you can die of the poison
that kills the beetle and the slug,
we must come again to worship you
on our knees, the common living dirt.

Toad dreams

That afternoon the dream of the toads rang through the elms by Little River and affected the thoughts of men, though they were not conscious that they heard it.

—Henry Thoreau

The dream of toads: we rarely
credit what we consider lesser
life with emotions big as ours,
but we are easily distracted,
abstracted. People sit nibbling,
before television's flicker watching
ghosts chase balls and each other
while the skunk is out risking grisly
death to cross the highway to mate;
while the fox scales the wire fence
where it knows the shotgun lurks
to taste the sweet blood of a hen.
Birds are greedy little bombs
bursting to give voice to appetite.
I had a cat who died of love, starving
when my husband left her too.
Dogs trail their masters across con-
tinents. We are far too busy
to be starkly simple in passion.
We will never dream the intense
wet spring lust of the toads.

Down at the bottom of things

In the marshes of the blood river
frogs blurt out their grocery lists
of lust, and some frogs croak poems.
In the brackish backwaters of the psyche
the strong night side of our nature
develops its food chain. I do believe
that in corporate board rooms, in bank
offices, in the subcommittees of Congress,
senators with oil bribes easing their way
toward power act from greed, yes,
but petty hatreds flash swarming thick
as piranhas in their murky speeches, and around
their deals musty resentments circle
buzzing like fat horseflies.

In the salty estuary of the blood river
small intermittent truths dart
in fear through the eel grass, and the nastier
facts come striding, herons stabbing
with long bills yet graceful when they rise in heavy
flight. Here we deal with the archaic base
of advertising slogans and bureaucratic
orders that condemn babies to kwashiorkor,
here on the mud flats of language. Our duty
rises red as the rusty moon, waxing
and waning surely but always returning.

Here where the salty fluids of the blood
meet the renewal of freshwater streaming
from the clouds soaked through the grasses,
down runoff ditches, wandering through brown
meanders of stream; here where the ocean
turns on its elbow muttering and begins
to heave back on itself, whispering
its rise in all the little fiddler crab
burrows, through all the interstices
of tidal grass, we read the news

in minute flotsam of the large
catastrophes out at sea and upriver.
The oil slicks, the wrecks, the sewage
tainted, the chemicals dumped in the stream
we taste here clamlike as we strain
the waters to prophesy in frogs' tongues.

A marsh smells like sex and teems
with tiny life that all the showier
big creatures of the shallow sea
fatten on. Here the only decision
that presents itself is to see, to watch,
to taste, to listen, to know and to say,
all with care as the heron stalks probing,
all with care as the crab scuttles into the safety
of burrow, all with care as the kingfisher
watches, one way the fish, the other way
the hawk. To survive saying, to say again
and again, here in the rich soup of creation,
in the obscure salty pit where the rhythms
of life repeat and renew, and the cost
of greed is etched in poison on every cell.

A story wet as tears

Remember the princess who kissed the frog
so he became a prince? At first they danced
all weekend, toasted each other in the morning
with coffee, with champagne at night
and always with kisses. Perhaps it was
in bed after the first year had ground
around she noticed he had become cold
with her. She had to sleep
with heating pad and down comforter.
His manner grew increasingly chilly
and damp when she entered a room.
He spent his time in water sports,
hydroponics, working on his insect
collection.

       Then in the third year
when she said to him one day, "My dearest,
are you taking your vitamins daily,
you look quite green," he leaped
away from her.

       Finally on their
fifth anniversary she confronted him.
"My precious, don't you love me any
more?" He replied, "Ribbit. Ribbit."
Though courtship turns frogs into princes,
marriage turns them quietly back.

Absolute zero in the brain

Penfield the great doctor did a lobotomy
on his own sister and recorded
pages of clinical observations
on her lack of initiative afterward.

Dullness, he wrote, is superseded
by euphoria at times. Slight hemi-
paresis with aphasia. The rebellious sister
died from the head down into the pages

of medical journals and Penfield founded
a new specialty. Intellectuals
sneer at moviegoers who confuse
Dr. Frankenstein with his monster.

The fans think Frankenstein is the monster.
Isn't he?

Eating my tail

There are times in my life to which I
return like a cat scratching, licking,
worrying at an old sore, a long since
exterminated nest of fleas behind my ear.
I seem sure that if I keep poking
and rubbing that old itch will finally
be quelled. Or is it pattern I seek?
A mapmaker returning to the mountains
to pace out again the distances.
Of course, if the massacre had not
occurred in this pass, why would we care?

Some disasters alter the landscape
and realign even the roads driven
over years before. It is the bloody
moon of pain that gives a lurid
backlighting to this scene I peer at
beating my wings of anxiety silent
as a bat. Yet if pain gives portent
to the words spoken, it denies entrance.

They sit at the table and eat. Wine
is poured, she gets up to bring
warm bread. Yellow apples are heaped
in an orange bowl whose sides reflect
candle flames. Telling a story, she takes
his hand. I know of course what she thinks
is happening and how wrong she is.

But if I opened his forehead, would I find
the violence and anger to come? The past,
it's turning out the pocket of a jacket
I wore in the garden: plant ties, half
a packet of seeds, a mummified peach:

a combination of intention and waste.
They laugh heartily and the soup steams
and the golden apples shine like lumps of amber.

The present tears at the past as if living
were something the mind could ever hold
like water in a cup or a map in the hand.
Maps are abstractions useful for finding
whatever is actually entered on them.
Otherwise you just walk in. And through.
When you go back it's always someplace else.

It breaks

You hand me a cup of water;
I drink it and thank you pretending
what I take into me so calmly
could not kill me. We take food
from strangers, from restaurants
behind whose swinging doors flies
swarm and settle, from estranged
lovers who dream over the salad plates
of breaking the bones of our backs.

Trust flits through the apple
blossoms, a tiny spring warbler
in bright mating plumage. Trust
relies on learned pattern
and signal to let us walk down
stairs without thinking each
step, without stumbling.

I take parts of your body
inside me. I give you
the flimsy black lace and sweat
stained sleaze of my secrets.
I lay my sleeping body naked
at your side. Jump, you shout.
I do and you catch me.

In love we open wide as a house
to a summer afternoon, every shade up
and window cranked open and doors
flung back to the probing breeze.
If we love long, we stand like row
houses with no outer walls.

Suddenly we are naked.
The plaster of bedrooms
hangs exposed, wallpaper

pink and beige skins of broken
intimacy, torn and flapping.

To fear you is fearing my left hand
cut off. The lineaments of old
desire remain, but the gestures
are new and harsh. Words unheard
before are spat out grating
with the rush of loosed anger.

Friends bear banner headlines
of your rewriting of our common
past. I wonder at my own trust
how absolute it was, part of me
like the bones of my pelvis.
You were the true center of my
cycles, the magnetic north
I used to plot my wanderings.

It is not that I will not love
again or give myself into partnership
or lie naked sweating secrets
like nectar, but I will never
share a joint checking account
and when some lover tells me, Always,
baby, I'll be thinking, sure,
until this one too meets an heiress
and ships out. After a bone breaks
you can see in X-rays
the healing and the damage.

What's that smell in the kitchen?

All over America women are burning dinners.
It's lambchops in Peoria; it's haddock
in Providence; it's steak in Chicago;
tofu delight in Big Sur; red
rice and beans in Dallas.
All over America women are burning
food they're supposed to bring with calico
smiles on platters glittering like wax.
Anger sputters in her brainpan, confined
but spewing out missiles of hot fat.
Carbonized despair presses like a clinker
from a barbecue against the back of her eyes.
If she wants to grill anything, it's
her husband spitted over a slow fire.
If she wants to serve him anything
it's a dead rat with a bomb in its belly
ticking like the heart of an insomniac.
Her life is cooked and digested,
nothing but leftovers in Tupperware.
Look, she says, once I was roast duck
on your platter with parsley but now I am Spam.
Burning dinner is not incompetence but war.

The weight

1.

I lived in the winter drought of his anger,
cold and dry and bright. I could not breathe.
My sinuses bled. Whatever innocent object
I touched, doorknob or light switch,
sparks leapt to my hand in shock.
Any contact could give sudden sharp pain.

2.

All too long I have been carrying a weight
balanced on my head: a large iron pot
supposed to hold something. Only now
when I have been forced to put it down,
do I find it empty except for a gritty stain
on the bottom. You have told me
this exercise was good for my posture.
Why then did my back always ache?

3.

All too often I have wakened at night
with that weight crouched on my chest,
an attack dog pinning me down. I would
open my eyes and see its eyes glowing
like the grates of twin coal furnaces
in red and hot menacing regard.
A low growl sang in its chest, vibrating
into my chest and belly its warning.

4.

If it rained for three weeks in August,
you knew I had caused it by weeping.
If your paper was not accepted, I had
corrupted the judges or led you astray
into beaches, dinner parties and cleaning
the house when you could have been working
an eighteen-hour day. If a woman would not
return the importunate pressure of your hand
on her shoulder, it was because I was watching
or because you believed she thought I

was watching. My watching and my looking away
equally displeased. Whatever I gave you
was wrong. It did not cost enough;
it cost too much. It was too fancy, for
that week you were a revolutionary
trekking on dry bread salted with sweat
and rhetoric. It was too plain; that week
you were the superb connoisseur whose palate
could be struck like a tuning fork only
by the perfect, to sing its true note.

5.

Wife was a box you kept pushing me down
into like a trunk crammed to overflowing
with off-season clothes, whose lid
you must push on to shut. You sat
on my head. You sat on my belly.
I kept leaking out like laughing
gas and you held your nose
lest I infect you with outrageous joy.

Gradually you lowered all the tents
of our pleasures and stowed them away.
We could not walk together in dunes or
marsh. No talk or travel. You would only fuck
in one position on alternate Thursdays
if the moon was in the right ascendancy.
Go and do with others all the things
you told me we could not afford.

Your anger was a climate I inhabited
like a desert in dry frigid weather
of high thin air and ivory sun,
sand dunes the wind lifted into stinging
clouds that blinded and choked me,
where my flesh froze to black ice.

Very late July

July in the afternoon, the sky
rings, a crystal goblet without a crack.
One gull passes over mewing for company.
A tiger swallowtail hovers near magenta
phlox, while a confetti cloud
of fritillaries covers the goldenglow.
Half under the tent of my skirt, my cat
blinks at the day, content watching,
allowing the swallowtail to light
within paw reach, purring too softly
to be heard, only the vibration from his
brown chest buzzing into my palm.
Among the scarlet blossoms of the runner
beans twining on their tripods
the hummingbird darts like a jet fighter.

Today in think tanks, the data analysts
not on vacation are playing war games.
A worker is packing plutonium by remote
control into new warheads. An adviser
is telling a president as they golf,
we could win it. July without a crack
as we live inside the great world egg.

Mornings in various years

1.

To wake and see the day piled up
before me like dirty dishes: I have
lived years knitting a love that
he would unravel, as if Penelope
spent every night making a warm
sweater that Odysseus would tear
in his careless diurnal anger.

2.

Waking alone I would marshal my tasks
like battalions of wild geese to bear me
up on the wings of duty over
the checkered fields of other lives.
Breakfast was hardest. I would trip
on ghostly shards of broken
domestic routines that entangled
my cold ankles as the cats yowled
to be fed, and so did I.

3.

I wake with any two cats, victors
of the nightly squabble of who
sleeps where, and beside me, you,
your morning sleepyhead big as a field
pumpkin, sleep caught in your fuzzy
hair like leaves. The sun pours in
sweet as orange juice or the rain licks
the windows with its tongue or the snow
softly packs the house in cotton batting.
This opal dawn glows from the center
as we both open our eyes and reach out
asking, are you there? You! You're
there, the unblemished day before us
like a clean white ironstone platter
waiting to be filled.

Digging in

This fall you will taste carrots
you planted, you thinned, you mulched,
you weeded and watered.
You don't know yet how sweet
they will taste, how yours.
This earth is yours as you love it.

We drink the water of this hill
and give our garbage to its soil.
We haul thatch for it and seaweed.
Out of it rise supper and roses
for the bedroom and herbs
for your next cold.

Your flesh grows out of this hill
like the maple trees. Its sweetness
is baked by this sun. Your eyes
have taken in sea and the light leaves
of the locust and the dark bristles
of the pine.

When we work in the garden you say
that now it feels sexual, the plants
pushing through us, the shivering
of the leaves. As we make love
later the oaks bend over us,
the hill listens.

The cats come and sit on the foot
of the bed to watch us.
Afterward they purr.
The tomatoes grow faster and the beans.
You are learning to live in circles
as well as straight lines.

The working writer

I admire you to tantrums they say,
you're so marvelously productive,
those plump books in litters
like piglets.

Then the comments light on my face
stinging like tiny wasps,
busy-busy, rush-rush, such a steamy
pressured life. Why don't
you take a week off
when I visit? I spend July
at the beach myself. August
I go to Maine. Martinique
in January. I keep in shape
Thursdays at the exercise salon.
Every morning I do yoga for two
hours; it would mellow you.
Then I grind wheat berries
for bread, weave macrame hammocks
and whip up a fluffy mousseline dress.
Oh, you buy your clothes.

I just don't know how you live
with weeds in the living room,
piles of papers so high the yellow
snow on top is perennial. Books
in the shower, books in bed,
a freezer full of books.
You need a cleaning lady or two.
I saw a bat in the bedroom
last night, potatoes flowering
behind the toilet.

My cats clean the house, I say.
I have them almost trained.
In winter we dig the potatoes.
All year we eat the books.

The back pockets of love

Your toes:
   modest stalagmites
      sticking up in the ice caves
      of the winter bed.

Your toes:
   succulent mushrooms,
      stumpy chimney pots
      rising in their row.

Wee round faces
   anonymous as nuns,
      callused, worn as coolies
         aging in their traces.

Small fry,
   wriggling moonbeam
      minnows escaped from the dark
         traps of your shoes.

Pipsqueak puppets,
   piglets nosing,
      soft thimbles, dumpy
         sofa pillows of flesh.

Love dwells in the major caves of the psyche,
chewing on the long bones of the limbs of courage,
the great haunches of resolution,
sucking the marrow bones, caves lit
by the lasting flames of the intellect,

but love cherishes too the back pockets,
the pencil ends of childhood fears,
the nose picking and throbbing sweet tooth,
the silly hardworking toes that curl
now blamelessly as dwarf cats
in the tousled nest of mutual morning bed.

Snow, snow

Like the sun on February ice dazzling;
like the sun licking the snow back
roughly so objects begin to poke through,
logs and steps, withered clumps of herb;
like the torch of the male cardinal
borne across the clearing from pine
to pine and then lighting among the bird
seed and bread scattered; like the sharp
shinned hawk gliding over the rabbit
colored marsh grass, exulting
in talon-hooked cries to his larger mate;
like the little pale green seedlings sticking
up their fragile heavy heads on white stalks
into the wide yellow lap of the pregnant sun;
like the sky of stained glass the eye seeks
for respite from the glitter that makes the lips
part; similar to all of these pleasures
of the failing winter and the as yet unbroken
blue egg of spring is our joy as we twist
and twine about each other in the bed
facing the window where the sun plays
the tabla of the thin cold air
and the snow sings soprano
and the emerging earth drones bass.

In which she begs (like everybody else) that love may last

The lilac blooms now in May,
our bed awash with its fragrance,
while beside the drive, buds
of peony and poppy swell
toward cracking, slivers of color
bulging like a flash of eye
from someone pretending to sleep.
Each in its garden slot, each
in its season, crocus gives way
to daffodil, through to fall
monkshood and chrysanthemum.
Only I am the wicked rose
that wants to bloom all year.
I am never replete with loving
you. Satisfaction
makes me greedy. I want
to blossom out with my joy of you
in March, in July, in October.
I want to drop my red red
petals on the hard black ice.

Let us gather at the river

I am the woman who sits by the river
river of tears
river of sewage
river of rainbows.
I sit by the river and count the corpses
floating by from the war upstream.
I sit by the river and watch the water
dwindle and the banks poke out like sore gums.
I watch the water change from green to shit brown.
I sit by the river and fish for your soul.
I want to lick it clean.
I want to turn it into a butterfly
that will weave drunkenly from orchid to rose.

Oh, close your eyes tight and push hard
and evolve, all together now. We can
do it if we try. We can take our world
back if we want. It's an araucana
egg, all blue and green
swaddled in filmy clouds.
Don't let them cook and gobble it,
azure and jungle green egg laid
by the extinct phoenix of the universe.

Send me your worn hacks of tired themes,
your dying horses of liberation,
your poor bony mules of freedom now.
I am the woman sitting by the river.
I mend old rebellions and patch them new.

Now the river turns from shit brown to bubbling blood
as an arm dressed in a uniform
floats by like an idling log.
Up too high to see, bombers big as bowling alleys

streak over and the automated battlefield
lights up like a Star Wars pinball machine.

I am the old woman sitting by the river scolding corpses.
I want to stare into the river and see the bottom
glinting like clean hair.
I want to outlive my usefulness
and sing water songs, songs
in praise of the green brown river
flowing clean through the blue green world.

Ashes, ashes, all fall down

1.

We walk on the earth and feed of it;
we breathe in the air or we choke;
we drink water or die, but you:
you cannot enter us. No pain
is like your touch.

Once we lived wholly without you,
plucking fruit, digging roots, shaking
down nuts, scavenging like bears.
Our cousin mammals ignore or flee
your angry lion's roar.

Emblem of all we have seized upon
in nature, energy made property,
as what we use uses us; what
we depend on enslaves us; what
we live by kills us.

We stretch out our hands to the fire
place watching the colors shift
until the mind gives up buried images
like the secret blue in the log
the flame unlocks.

2.

Burning, burning, that fall I galloped,
the cries of torn children ringing
in my skull. Even cats mating in my Brooklyn
alley invoked images of thatched villages
scorched by bombing.

Burning, burning, I turned and roared
simple, loud as a trumpet blown, sonorous,
brassy, commanded and commanding. In that

heat everything dried from the inside,
baked to ashes.

Passion simplifies like surgery.
We burn, and what we burn are the books,
the couch, the rug, the bed, the houseplants,
the friends who can't clear out
fast enough.

Yet a passionless life: all the virtues
gilded like saints in their niches
and nothing to move them. The architecture
of airports, laundromats. Cafeteria food
for the tepid will.

On one hand hopping along, a well-appointed
portly toad licking up bugs, patrolling
the garden. On the other, flying
through the night like a skunked dog,
howling and drooling.

Burning, burning, we can't live
in the fire. Nor can we in ice.
Long ago we wandered from our homeland
tropics following game to these harsh
but fertile shores.

3.

On solstices, our ancestors leapt
through fire, to bring the sun around.
Surely some were not nimble enough
and a trailing scarf or skirt turned
burning shroud.

Without risk maybe the sun won't return.
Without risk gradually the temperature
drops, slowly, slowly. One day you notice
the roses have all died. The next year
no corn ripens.

Then even the wheat rots where it stands.
Glaciers slide down the mountains
choking the valleys. The birds are gone.

On the north side of the heart, the snow
never melts.

When I stare into fire, I see figures
dancing. People of our merry potlatch,
ghosts, demons or simply the memory
of times I have danced in ecstasy all night,
my hair on fire.

5.

Even breathing is a little burning.
The banked fire of the cells eats
oxygen like the arsonist's blaze.
All the minute furnaces stoked inside
warm our skin.

Life is a burning, and what we burn
is all the others we eat and drink.
We burn the carrot, we burn the cow,
we burn the calf, we burn the peach,
we burn the wine.

Life is a burning, and what we burn
is ourselves. Observe the back begin
to curl, to bow like a paper match
consumed, and the dark hair powdering
to grey ashes.

You are all we cannot live with
or without. You warm and you spoil,
you heat and you kill. Like us
whatever you touch, you seize for your use
and use up.

from
My Mother's Body

Putting the good things away

In the drawer were folded fine
batiste slips embroidered with scrolls
and posies, edged with handmade
lace too good for her to wear.

Daily she put on schmattehs
fit only to wash the car
or the windows, rags
that had never been pretty

even when new: somewhere
such dresses are sold only
to women without money to waste
on themselves, on pleasure,

to women who hate their bodies,
to women whose lives close on them.
Such clothes come bleached by tears,
packed in salt like herring.

Yet she put the good things away
for the good day that must surely
come, when promises would open
like tulips their satin cups

for her to drink the sweet
sacramental wine of fulfillment.
The story shone in her as through
tinted glass, how the mother

gave up and did without
and was in the end crowned
with what? scallions? crowned
queen of the dead place

in the heart where old dreams
whistle on bone flutes,
where run-over pets are forgotten,
where lost stockings go?

In the coffin she was beautiful
not because of the undertaker's
garish cosmetics but because
that face at eighty was still

her face at eighteen peering
over the drab long dress
of poverty, clutching a book.
Where did you read your dreams, Mother?

Because her expression softened
from the pucker of disappointment,
the grimace of swallowed rage,
she looked a white-haired girl.

The anger turned inward, the anger
turned inward, where
could it go except to make pain?
It flowed into me with her milk.

Her anger annealed me.
I was dipped into the cauldron
of boiling rage and rose
a warrior and a witch

but still vulnerable
there where she held me.
She could always wound me
for she knew the secret places.

She could always touch me
for she knew the pressure
points of pleasure and pain.
Our minds were woven together.

I gave her presents and she hid
them away, wrapped in plastic.
Too good, she said, too good.
I'm saving them. So after her death

I sort them, the ugly things
that were sufficient for every
day and the pretty things for which
no day of hers was ever good enough.

They inhabit me

I am pregnant with certain deaths
of women who choked before they
could speak their names
could know their names
before they had names to know.

I am owl, the spirit said,
I swim through the darkness on wide wings.
I see what is behind me
as well as what is before.
In the morning a splash of blood

on the snow marks where I found
what I needed. In the mild
light of day the crows mob
me, cursing. Are you the daughter
of my amber clock-tower eyes?

I am pregnant with certain deaths
of women whose hands were replaced
by paper flowers, which must be kept
clean, which could tear on a glance,
which could not hold even water.

I am cat. I rub your prejudices
against the comfortable way they grow.
I am fastidious, not as a careful
housewife, but as a careful lover,
keeping genitals as clean as face.

I turn up my belly of warm sensuality
to your fingers, purring my pleasure
and letting my claws just tip out.
Are you the daughter of the fierce
aria of my passion scrawled on the night?

I am pregnant with certain deaths
of women who dreamed that the lover
would strike like lightning and throw

them over the saddle and carry them off.
It was the ambulance that came.

I am wolf. I call across the miles
my messages of yearning and hunger,
and the snow speaks to me constantly
of food and want and friend and foe.
The iron air is heavy with ice

tweaking my nose and the sound
of the wind is sharp and whetted.
Commenting, chatting, calling,
we run through the net of scents
querying, Are you my daughter?

I am pregnant with deaths of certain
women who curled, wound in the skeins
of dream, who secreted silk
from spittle and bound themselves
in swaddling clothes of shrouds.

I am raccoon. I thrive in woods,
I thrive in the alleys of your cities.
With my little hands I open
whatever you shut away from me.
On your garbage I grow glossy.

Among packs of stray dogs I bare
my teeth, and the warring rats part.
I flourish like the ailanthus tree;
in your trashheaps I dig underground
castles. Are you my daughter?

I am pregnant with certain deaths
of women who wander slamming doors
and sighing as if to be overheard,
talking to themselves like water left
running, tears dried to table salt.

They hide in my hair like crabs,
they are banging on the nodes of my spine
as on the door of a tardy elevator.
They want to ride up to the observation
platform and peer out my eyes for the view.

All this wanting creates a black hole
where ghosts and totems whirl and join
passing through into antimatter of art,
the alternate universe in which such certain
deaths as theirs and mine throb with light.

Unbuttoning

The buttons lie jumbled in a tin
that once held good lapsang souchong
tea from China, smoky as the smell
from a woodstove in the country,
leaves opening to flavor and fate.

As I turn buttons over, they sound
like strange money being counted
toward a purchase as I point
dumbly in a foreign bazaar,
coins pittering from my hand.

Buttons are told with the fingers
like worry beads as I search
the trove for something small
and red to fill the missing
slot on a blouse placket.

I carried them from my mother's
sewing table, a wise legacy
not only practical but better
able than fading snapshots
to conjure buried seasons.

Button stamped with an anchor
means my grade-school peacoat.
Button in the form of a white
daisy from a sky blue dress
she wore, splashed with that flower,

rouses her face like a rosy dahlia
bent over me petaled with curls.
O sunflower hungry for joy
who turned her face through the years
bleak, withered, still yearning.

The tea was a present I brought
her from New York where she
had never gone and never would.
This mauve nub's from a dress
once drenched in her blood;

this, from a coral dress she wore
the day she taught me that word,
summer '41, in Florida:
"Watch the clipper ships take off
for Europe. Soon war will come to us."

"They will not rise so peacefully
for years. Over there they're
killing us and nobody cares.
Remember always. Coral is built
of bodies of the dead piled up."

Buttons are useful little monuments.
They fasten and keep decently
shut and warm. They also open.
Rattling in my hand, they're shells
left by vanished flesh.

Out of the rubbish

Among my mother's things I found
a bottle-cap flower: the top
from a ginger ale
into which had been glued
crystalline beads from a necklace
surrounding a blue bauble.

It is not unattractive,
this star-shaped posy
in the wreath of fluted
aluminum, but it is not
as a thing of beauty
that I carried it off.

A receeding vista opens
of working-class making do:
the dress that becomes
a blouse that becomes
a dolldress, potholders,
rags to wash windows.

Petunias in the tire.
Remnants of old rugs
laid down over the holes
in rugs that had once
been new when the rem-
nants were first old.

A three-inch birchbark
canoe labelled Muskegon,
small wooden shoes, souvenirs
of Holland, Michigan,
an ashtray from the Blue Hole
reputed bottomless.

Look out the window
at the sulfur sky.
The street is grey as
newspapers. Rats
waddle up the alley.
The air is brown.

If we make curtains
of the rose bedecked table
cloth, the stain won't show
and it will be cheerful,
cheerful. Paint it primrose.
Paint it turquoise, lime.

How I used to dream
in Detroit of deep cobalt,
of ochre reds, of cadmium
yellow. I dreamed of sea
and burning sun, of red
islands and blue volcanos.

After she washed the floors
she used to put down newspapers
to keep them clean. When
the newspapers had become
dirty, the floor beneath
was no longer clean.

In the window, ceramic
bunnies sprouted cactus.
A burro offered fuchsia.
In the hat, a wandering Jew.
"That was your grandfather.
He spoke nine languages."

"Don't you ever want to
travel?" "I did when I
was younger. Now, what
would be the point?
Who would want to meet me?
I'd be ashamed."

One night alone she sat
at her kitchen table
gluing baubles in a cap.
When she had finished,
pleased she hid it away
where no one could see.

My mother's body

The dark socket of the year
the pit, the cave where the sun lies down
and threatens never to rise,
when despair descends softly as the snow
covering all paths and choking roads:

then hawkfaced pain seized you
threw you so you fell with a sharp
cry, a knife tearing a bolt of silk.
My father heard the crash but paid
no mind, napping after lunch

yet fifteen hundred miles north
I heard and dropped a dish.
Your pain sunk talons in my skull
and crouched there cawing, heavy
as a great vessel filled with water,

oil or blood, till suddenly next day
the weight lifted and I knew your mind
had guttered out like the Hanukkah
candles that burn so fast, weeping
veils of wax down the hanukiyah.

Those candles were laid out,
friends invited, ingredients bought
for latkes and apple pancakes,
that holiday for liberation
and the winter solstice

when tops turn like little planets.
Shall you have all or nothing
take half or pass by untouched?
Nothing you got, *Shin* said the dreidl
as the room stopped spinning.

The angel folded you up like laundry
your body thin as an empty dress.
Your clothes were curtains
hanging on the window of what had
been your flesh and now was glass.

Outside in Florida shopping plazas
loudspeakers blared Christmas carols
and palm trees were decked with blinking
lights. Except by the tourist
hotels, the beaches were empty.

Pelicans with pregnant pouches
flapped overhead like pterodactyls.
In my mind I felt you die
First the pain lifted and then
you flickered and went out.

2.

I walk through the rooms of memory.
Sometimes everything is shrouded in dropcloths,
every chair ghostly and muted.

Other times memory lights up from within
bustling scenes acted just the other side
of a scrim through which surely I could reach

my fingers tearing at the flimsy curtain
of time which is and isn't and will be
the stuff of which we're made and unmade.

In sleep the other night I met you, seventeen
your first nasty marriage just annulled,
thin from your abortion, clutching a book

against your cheek and trying to look
older, trying to look middle class,
trying for a job at Wanamaker's

dressing for parties in cast off
stage costumes of your sisters. Your eyes
were hazy with dreams. You did not

notice me waving as you wandered
past and I saw your slip was showing.
You stood still while I fixed your clothes,

as if I were your mother. Remember me
combing your springy black hair, ringlets
that seemed metallic, glittering;

remember me dressing you, my seventy-year-
old mother who was my last dollbaby,
giving you too late what your youth had wanted.

3.

What is this mask of skin we wear,
what is this dress of flesh,
this coat of few colors and little hair?

This voluptuous seething heap of desires
and fears squeaking, mice turned up
in a steaming haystack with their babies?

This coat has been handed down, an heirloom:
this coat of black hair and ample flesh,
this coat of pale slightly ruddy skin.

This set of hips and thighs, these buttocks
they provided cushioning for my grandmother
Hannah, for my mother Bert and for me

those major muscles by which we walk
and walk and walk over the hard earth
in search of peace and plenty.

My mother is my mirror and I am hers.
What do we see? Our face grown young again,
our breasts grown firm, legs lean and elegant.

Our arms quivering with fat, eyes
set in the bark of wrinkles, hands puffy,
belly seamed with childbearing,

Give me your dress that I might try it on.
Oh it will not fit you mother, you are too fat.
I will not fit you mother.

I will not be the bride you can dress,
the obedient dutiful daughter you would chew,
a dog's leather bone to sharpen your teeth.

You strike me sometimes just to hear the sound.
Loneliness turns your fingers into hooks
barbed and drawing blood with their caress.

My twin, my sister, my lost love,
I carry you in me like an embryo
as once you carried me.

4.

What is it we turn from, what is it we fear?
Did I truly think you could put me back inside?
Did I think I would fall into you as into a molten
furnace and be recast, that I would become you?

What did you fear in me, the child who wore
your hair, the woman who let that black hair
grow long as a banner of darkness, when you
a proper flapper wore yours cropped.

You pushed and you pulled on my rubbery
flesh, you kneaded me like a ball of dough.
Rise, rise, and then you pounded me flat.
Secretly bones formed in the bread.

I became willful, private as a cat.
You never knew what alleys I had wandered.
You called me bad and I posed like a gutter
queen in a dress sewn of knives.

All I feared was being stuck in a box
with a lid. A good woman appeared to me

indistinguishable from a dead one
except that she worked all the time.

Your payday never came. Your dreams ran
with bright colors like Mexican cottons
that bled onto the drab sheets of the day
and would not bleach with scrubbing.

My dear, what you said was one thing
but what you sang was another, sweetly
subversive and dark as blackberries
and I became the daughter of your dream.

This body is your body, ashes now
and roses, but alive in my eyes, my breasts,
my throat, my thighs. You run in me
a tang of salt in the creek waters of my blood,

you sing in my mind like wine. What you
did not dare in your life you dare in mine.

How grey, how wet, how cold

They are bits of fog caught in armor.
The outside pretends to the solidity of rocks
and requires force and skill bearing in
to cut the muscle, shatter the illusion.

If you stare at them, your stomach
curls, the grey eyes of Athena
pried out, the texture of heavy phlegm,
chill clots of mortality and come.

They lie on the tongue, distillations
of the sea. Fresh as the morning
wind that tatters the mist.
Sweet as cream but with that bottom

of granite, the taste of deep well
water drawn up on the hottest day,
the vein of slate in true Chablis,
the kiss of acid sharpening the tongue.

They slip down quick as minnows
darting to cover, and the mouth
remembers sex. Both provide
a meeting of the primitive

and worldly, in that we do
little more for oysters than the gull
smashing the shells on the rocks
or the crab wrestling them open,

yet in subtle flavor and the choice
to taste them raw comes a delicacy
not of the brain but of the senses
and the wit to leave perfection bare.

Taking a hot bath

Surely nobody has ever decided
to go on a diet while in a tub.
The body is beautiful stretched
out under water wavering.

It suggests a long island of pleasure
whole seascapes of calm sensual
response, the nerves as gentle fronds
of waterweed swaying in warm currents.

Then if ever we must love ourselves
in the amniotic fluid floating
a ship at anchor in a perfect
protected blood-warm tropical bay.

The water enters us and the minor
pains depart, supplanted guests,
the aches, the strains, the chills.
Muscles open like hungry clams.

Born again from my bath like a hot
sweet tempered, sweet smelling baby,
I am ready to seize sleep like a milky breast
or start climbing my day hand over hand.

Sleeping with cats

I am at once source
and sink of heat; giver
and taker. I am a vast
soft mountain of slow breathing.
The smells I exude soothe them:
the lingering odor of sex,
of soap, even of perfume,
its afteraroma sunk into skin
mingling with sweat and the traces
of food and drink.

They are curled into flowers
of fur, they are coiled
hot seashells of flesh
in my armpit, around my head
a dark sighing halo.
They are plastered to my side,
a poultice fixing sore muscles
better than a heating pad.
They snuggle up to my sex
purring. They embrace my feet.

Some cats I place like a pillow.
In the morning they rest where
I arranged them, still sleeping.
Some cats start at my head
and end between my legs
like a textbook lover. Some
slip out to prowl the living room
patrolling, restive, then
leap back to fight about
hegemony over my knees.

Every one of them cares
passionately where they sleep

and with whom.
Sleeping together is a euphemism
for people but tantamount
to marriage for cats.
Mammals together we snuggle
and snore through the cold nights
while the stars swing round
the pole and the great horned
owl hunts for flesh like ours.

The place where everything changed

Great love is an abrupt switching
in a life bearing along at express speeds
expecting to reach the designated stations
at the minute listed in the timetable.

Great love can cause derailment,
coaches upended, people screaming,
luggage strewn over the mountainside,
blood and paper on the grass.

It's months before the repairs are done,
everyone discharged from the hospital,
all the lawsuits settled, damage
paid for, the scandal subsided.

Then we get on with the journey
in some new direction, hiking overland
with camels, mules, via helicopter
by barge through canals.

The maps are all redrawn and what
was north is east of south
and there be dragons in those mountains
and the sun shines warmer and hairier

and the moon has a cat's face.
There is more sunshine. More rain.
The seasons are marked and intense.
We seldom catch colds.

There is always you at my back
ready to fight when I must fight;
there is always you at my side
the words flashing light and shadow.

What was grey ripples scarlet and golden;
what was bland reeks of ginger and brandy;

what was empty roars like a packed stadium;
what slept gallops for miles.

Even our bones are reformed in the close
night when we hold each other's dreams.
Memories uncoil backward and are remade.
Now the first egg itself is freshly twinned.

We build daily houses brick by brick.
We put each other up at night like tents.
This story tells itself as it grows.
Each morning we give birth to one another.

The chuppah

The chuppah stands on four poles.
The home has its four corners.
The chuppah stands on four poles.
The marriage stands on four legs.
Four points loose the winds
that blow on the walls of the house,
the south wind that brings the warm rain,
the east wind that brings the cold rain,
the north wind that brings the cold sun
and the snow, the long west wind
bringing weather off the far plains.

Here we live open to the seasons.
Here the winds caress and cuff us
contrary and fierce as bears.
Here the winds are caught and snarling
in the pines, a cat in a net clawing
breaking twigs to fight loose.
Here the winds brush your face
soft in the morning as feathers
that float down from a dove's breast.

Here the moon sails up out of the ocean
dripping like a just washed apple.
Here the sun wakes us like a baby.
Therefore the chuppah has no sides.

It is not a box.
It is not a coffin.
It is not a dead end.
Therefore the chuppah has no walls.
We have made a home together
open to the weather of our time
We are mills that turn in the winds of struggle
converting fierce energy into bread.

The canopy is the cloth of our table
where we share fruit and vegetables
of our labor, where our care for the earth
comes back and we take its body in ours.

The canopy is the cover of our bed
where our bodies open their portals wide,
where we eat and drink the blood
of our love, where the skin shines red
as a swallowed sunrise and we burn
in one furnace of joy molten as steel
and the dream is flesh and flower.

O my love O my love we dance
under the chuppah standing over us
like an animal on its four legs,
like a table on which we set our love
as a feast, like a tent
under which we work
not safe but no longer solitary
in the searing heat of our time.

House built of breath

Words plain as pancakes syruped with endearment.
Simple as potatoes, homely as cottage cheese.

Wet as onions, dry as salt.
Slow as honey, fast as seltzer,

my raisin, my sultana, my apricot love
my artichoke, furry one, my pineapple

I love you daily as milk,
I love you nightly as aromatic port.

The words trail a bitter slime like slugs,
then in the belly warm like cabbage borscht.

The words are hung out on the line,
sheets for the wind to bleach.

The words are simmering slowly
on the back burner like a good stew.

Words are the kindling in the woodstove.
Even the quilt at night is stuffed with word down.

When we are alone the walls sing
and even the cats talk but only in Yiddish.

When we are alone we make love in deeds.
And then in words. And then in food.

Nailing up the mezuzah

A friend from Greece
brought a tin house
on a plaque, designed
to protect our abode,
as in Greek churches
embossed legs or hearts
on display entreat aid.
I hung it but now
nail my own proper charm.

I refuse no offers of help,
at least from friends,
yet this presence
is long overdue. Mostly
we nurture our own
blessings or spoil them,
build firmly or undermine
our walls. Who are termites
but our obsessions gnawing?

Still the winds blow hard
from the cave of the sea
carrying off what they will.
Our smaller luck abides
like a worm snug in an apple
who does not comprehend
the shivering of the leaves
as the ax bites hard
in the smooth trunk.

We need all help proffered
by benign forces. Outside
we commit our beans to the earth,
the tomato plants started
in February to the care
of the rain. My little
pregnant grey cat offers
the taut bow of her belly
to the sun's hot tongue.

Saturday I watched alewives
swarm in their thousands
waiting in queues quivering
pointed against the white
rush of the torrents
to try their leaps upstream.
The gulls bald as coffin
nails stabbed them casually
conversing in shrieks, picnicking.

On its earth, this house
is oriented. We grow
from our bed rooted firmly
as an old willow into the water
of our dreams flowing deep
in the hillside. This hill
is my temple, my soul.
Malach hamoves, angel of death
pass over, pass on.

The faithless

Sleep, you jade smooth liar,
you promised to come
to me, come to me
waiting here like a cut
open melon ripe as summer.

Sleep, you black velvet
tomcat, where are you prowling?
I set a trap of sheets
clean and fresh as daisies,
pillows like cloudy sighs.

Sleep, you soft-bellied
angel with feathered thighs,
you tease my cheek with the brush
of your wings. I reach
for you but clutch air.

Sleep, you fur-bottomed tramp,
when I want you, you're in
everybody's bed but my own.
Take you for granted and you stalk
me from the low point of every hour.

Sleep, omnivorous billy goat,
you gobble the kittens, the crows,
the cop on duty, the fast horse,
but me you leave on the plate
like a cold shore dinner.

Is this divorce permanent?
Runneled with hope I lie down
nightly longing to pass
again under the fresh blessing
of your weight and broad wings.

And whose creature am I?

At times characters from my novels swarm through me,
children of my mind, and possess me as dybbuks.
My own shabby memories they have plucked and eaten
till sometimes I cannot remember my own sorrows.
In all that I value there is a core of mystery,
in the seed that wriggles its new roots into the soil
and whose pale head bursts the surface,
in the dance where our bodies merge and reassemble,
in the starving baby whose huge glazing eyes
burned into my bones, in the look that passes
between predator and prey before the death blow.

I know of what rags and bones and clippings
from frothing newsprint and poisonous glue
my structures are built. Yet these creatures
I have improvised like golem walk off and thrive.
Between one and two thirds of our lives we spend
in darkness, and the little lights we turn on
make little holes in that great thick rich void.
We are never done with knowing or with gnawing,
but under the saying is whispering, touching
and silence. Out of a given set of atoms
we cast and recast the holy patterns new.

Magic mama

The woman who shines with a dull comfortable glow.
The woman who sweats honey, an aphid
enrolled to sweeten the lives of others.

The woman who puts down her work like knitting
the moment you speak, but somehow it gets done
secretly in the night while everyone sleeps.

The woman whose lap is wide as the Nile
delta, whose voice is a lullaby
whose flesh is stuffed with goosedown.

Whose eyes are soft-focus mirrors.
Whose arms are bolsters. Whose love
is laid on like the municipal water.

She is not the mother goddess, vortex
of dark and light powers with her consorts,
her hungers, her favorites, her temper

blasting the corn so it withers in its ear,
her bloody humor that sends the hunter fleeing
to be tracked and torn by his hounds,

the great door into the earth's darkness
where bones are rewoven into wheat,
who loves the hawk as she loves the rabbit.

Big mama has no power, not even over herself.
The taxpayer of guilt, whatever she gives
you both agree is never enough.

She is a one-way street down which pour
parades of opulent gifts and admiration
from a three-shift factory of love.

Magic mama has to make it right, straighten
the crooked, ease pain, raise the darkness,
feed the hungry and matchmake for the lonesome

and ask nothing in return. If you win
you no longer know her, and if you lose
it is because her goodness failed you.

Whenever you create big mama from another
woman's smile, a generosity of spirit working
like yeast in the inert matter of the day,

you are stealing from a woman her own ripe
sweet desire, the must of her fears,
the shadow she casts into her own future

and turning her into a diaper service,
the cleaning lady of your adventure.
Who thanks a lightbulb for giving light?

Listen, your mother is not your mother.
She is herself and unmothered. It is time
to take the apron off your mind.

Does the light fail us, or do we fail the light?

My old cat lives under a chair.
Her long fur conceals the sharp
jut of her fleshless bones.

Her eyes are dimmed by clouds
of cataract, visible only
if you remember their willow green

as I could judge my mother's
by calling up that fierce charred
brown gaze, smiting, searching.

When one of the young cats approaches
she growls in anger harmless
as distant thunder. They steal her food.

They do not act from malice.
They would curl up with her and wash.
She hisses fear. Her lifelong

companion died. They appeared.
Surely the young bear the blame
for all the changes that menace

in the fog of grey shapes looming.
Her senses that like new snow
had registered the brushstrokes

of tracks, the fall of a pine needle,
the alighting of a chickadee;
that tantalized her with message

of vole and shrew and rabbit,
boasting homage her lovers sprayed,
have failed her like an old

hanging bridge that decays
letting her drop through in terror
to the cold swift river beneath.

The light is trickling away.

2.

One day this week my father called
briefly emerging from the burrow
he bought himself lined with nurses.

He really wants to phone my mother.
Often he calls me by her name
but every time I fail him.

I am the dead woman in body,
hips and breasts and thighs,
elbows and chin and earlobes,

black black hair as at the age
she bore me, when he still
loved her, here she stands,

but when I open my mouth
it's the wrong year and the world
bristles with women who make short

hard statements like men and don't
apologize enough, who don't cry
when he yells or makes a fist.

He tells me I have stolen his stamps
down in Florida, the bad utopia
where he must share a television.

You took my nail scissors, he shouts
but means I stole his vigor
deposited in his checkbook like a giant's

external soul. I have his checkbook
and sign, power of attorney,
as I pay his doctors, doctors,

doctors, as I hunch with calculator
trying to balance accounts. We each
feel enslaved to the other's will.

3.

Father, I don't want your little pot
of nuggets secreted by bad living
hidden in the mattress of Merrill Lynch

in an account you haven't touched
for twenty years, stocks that soared,
plummeted, doddering along now

in their own mad dinosaur race.
That stock is the doctor that Mother
couldn't call when she had the first

stroke, the dress she didn't get,
at eighty-six still scrubbing, cooking,
toting heavy laundry. The dentist

I couldn't go to so I chewed
aspirin as my teeth broke
at fifteen when I went out to work.

The ghostly dust bowl roared in the mind
afterward, the desert of poverty
where you would surely perish and starve

if you did not hide away pennies of power,
make do, make do, hold hard,
build a fortress of petrified dollars

stuck together like papier-mâché
so the tempest of want
could be shut out to howl at others.

After she died, you bought Total Life Care,
a tower of middle-class comfort
where you could sit down to lunch

declaring, My broker says.
But nobody would listen. Only
Mother had to listen and she is dead.

You hid alone in your room fighting
with the cleaning woman who came
each week but didn't do it right,

then finally one midnight wandered out
naked to the world among rustling
palms demanding someone make you lunch.

4.

You mutter, this was supposed to be fun.
Do you see your future in the bent
ones who whimper into their laps,

who glare at walls through which
the faces of the absent peer, who hear
conspiracy mutter in the plumbing?

I am the bad daughter who could speak
with my mother's voice if I wanted,
because I wear her face, who ought

to be cooking your meals, who ought
to be running the vacuum you bought
her, but instead I pretend

I am married, pretend to be writing
books and giving speeches.
You won't forgive her ever for dying

but I heard you call the night nurse
by her name. Grey blows in
the fog that took Mother while you slept,

the fog that thickens between you
and strangers here where all
is provided and nothing is wanted.

The sun blasts on, flat and blatant.
Everything was built yesterday
but you. Nobody here remembers

the strike when you walked the picket line
joking with sleet freezing your hair,
how you stood against the flaming wall

of steel and found the cracked bearing,
how you alone could make the old turbines
turn over, how you had the wife

other men watched when she swayed
over the grass at the company picnic,
how you could drink them all witless.

You're a shadow swallowed by fog.
Through your eyes it enters your brain.
When it lifts you see only pastel

walls and then your anger standing there
gleaming like a four-hundred-horsepower car
you have lost your license to drive.

from
Available Light

Available light

Ripe and runny as perfect Brie, at this age
appetites mature rampant and allowed.
I am wet as a salt marsh under the flood tide
of the full solstice moon and dry as salt itself
that draws the superfluous juice from the tissues
to leave the desiccated butterfly wing intact.

I know myself as I know the four miles I walk
every morning, the sky like ice formed on skim
milk, the sky dappled and fat and rolling, never
the same two hours later. I know there are rooms
upon caverns opening off corridors I will never
enter, as well as those I'll be thrust into.

I am six with my mother watching Clippers
take off for Lisbon. I am nine and the President
whose voice is a personal god is dying in the radio.
I am twelve and coming while I mutter yes, yes,
of course, this is what the bones grow around to hold.
I am twenty-four as my best friend bleeds her life out.

At any moment I find myself under the water of my
past trying to breathe in that thick refracted medium.
At any moment a voice is speaking to me like a p.a.
system that one day amplifies a lecture on newts
and the next day jazz. I am always finding new
beings in me like otters swimming in the soup.

I have friends who gave themselves to Marx, to Freud,
to A.A., to Christianity or Buddhism or Goddess
religions, to the Party or the Lord or the Lover.
As a Jew, I have a god who returns me to myself
uncleaned, to be used again, since forgiveness must
be sung but changes not one needle falling from a pine.

As consequences show their lengthened teeth
from the receding gums, we hunger for the larger
picture, the longer view, and yet and yet
I cannot augment the natural curve of earth

except by including the moth and the mammoth,
the dark river percolating through the sea

built rock, the dense memories of shell
and sediment, the million deaths recorded
in each inch; the warm funky breath
of Leviathan as he breaches off the portside;
people in boots struggling to shove the pilot
whales free that a storm surge grounded.

In winter the light is red and short.
The sun hangs its wizened rosehip in the oaks.
By midafternoon night is folding in.
The ground is locked against us like a door.
Yet faces shine so the eyes stretch for them
and tracks in the snow are etched, calligraphy

I learn by rote and observation, patient
the way I am finally learning Hebrew
at fifty, forgiving my dead parents
who saw squinting by their own scanty light.
By four o'clock I must give up the woods,
come in, turn on every lamp to read.

Later when the moon has set I go out
and let the spears of Sirius and Rigel
pierce the ivory of my skull and enter
my blood like glowing isotopes of distance.
As I stand in the cold vault of the night
I see more and fainter stars as my eyes

clear or my blood cools. The barred owl
hoots. The skunk prances past me to stir
the compost pile with her sharp nails.
A lithe weasel flicks across the cul-de-sac.
Even the dead of winter: it seethes with more
than I can ever live to name and speak.

Joy Road and Livernois

My name was Pat. We used to read Poe in bed
till we heard blood dripping in the closet.
I fell in love with a woman who could ring
all bells of my bones tolling, jangling.
But she in her cape and her Caddy
had to shine in the eyes of the other pimps,
a man among monkeys, so she turned me on the streets
to strut my meek ass. To quiet my wailing
she taught me to slip the fire in my arm,
the white thunder rolling over till nothing
hurt but coming down. One day I didn't.
I was fifteen. My face gleamed in the casket.

My name was Evie. We used to shoplift,
my giggling, wide-eyed questions, your fast hands;
we picked up boys together on the corners.
The cops busted me for stealing, milled me,
sent me up for prostitution because I weren't
no virgin. I met my boyfriend in the courts.
Together we robbed a liquor store that wouldn't
sell us whiskey. I liked to tote a gun.
It was the cleanest thing I ever held.
It was the only power I ever had.
I could look any creep straight on in the eyes.
A state trooper blew my face off in Marquette.

My name was Peggy. Across the street from the gas-
works, my mom raised nine kids. My brother-
in-law porked me while my sister gave birth
choking me with the pillow when I screamed.
I got used to it. My third boyfriend knocked me up.
Now I've been pregnant for twenty years,
always a belly bigger than me to push around
like an overloaded wheelbarrow ready to spill
on the blacktop. Now it's my last one,
a tumor big as a baby when they found it.
When I look in the mirror I see my mom.

Remember how we braided each other's hair,
mine red, yours black. Now I'm bald
as an egg and nearly boiled through.

I was Teresa. I used to carry a long clasp
knife I stole from my uncle. Running nights
through the twitching streets, I'd finger it.
It made me feel as mean as any man.
My boyfriend worked on cars until they flew.
All those hot nights riding around and around
when we had no place to go but back.
Those hot nights we raced out on the highway
faster faster till the blood fizzed in my throat
like shaken soda. It shot in an arc
when he hit the pole and I went out the windshield,
the knife I showed you how to use, still
on its leather thong between my breasts
where it didn't save me from being cut in two.

I was Gladys. Like you, I stayed in school.
I did not lay down in backseats with boys.
I became a nurse, married, had three sons.
My ankles swelled. I worked the night hours
among the dying and accident cases. My husband
left me for a girl he met in a bar, left debts,
a five-year-old Chevy, a mortgage.
My oldest came home in a body bag. My youngest
ran off. The middle one drinks beer and watches
the soaps since the Kelsey-Hayes plant closed.
Then my boy began to call me from the alley.
Every night he was out there calling, Mama,
help me! It hurts, Mama! Take me home.
This is the locked ward and the drugs
eat out my head like busy worms.

With each of them I lay down, my twelve-
year-old scrawny tough body like weathered
wood pressed to their pain, and we taught
each other love and pleasure and ourselves.

We invented the places, the sounds, the smells,
the little names. At twelve I was violent
in love, a fiery rat, a whip snake,
a starving weasel, all teeth and speed
except for the sore fruit of my new breasts
pushing out. What did I learn? To value
my pleasure and how little the love of women
can shield against the acid city rain.

You surge among my many ghosts. I never think
I got out because I was smart, brave, hard-
working, attractive. Evie was brave.
Gladys and Teresa were smart. Peggy worked
sixteen hours. Pat gleamed like olivewood
polished to a burnish as if fire lived in wood.
I wriggled through an opening left just big enough
for one. There is no virtue in survival
only luck, and a streak of indifference
that I could take off and keep going.

I got out of those Detroit blocks where the air
eats stone and melts flesh, where jobs
dangle and you jump and jump. Where there are
more drugs than books, more ways to die
than ways to live, because I ran fast,
ran hard, and never stopped looking back.
It is not looking back that turned me
to salt, no, I taste my salt from the mines
under Detroit, the salt of our common juices.
Girls who lacked everything except trouble,
contempt and rough times, girls
used like urinals, you are the salt
keeps me from rotting as the years swell.
I am the fast train you are traveling in
to a world of a different color, and the love
we cupped so clumsily in our hands to catch
rages and drives onward, an engine of light.

Daughter of the African evolution

The beauty of the great predators amazes me,
the music of their sleek haunch muscles rippling,
the clear fierce gaze with the fire of hunger
dancing golden in those slitting pupils,
the way the hawk plays in the columns of air,
the snow leopard balances leaps with her heavy
tail among the rocks.

The grace of the fast grazers dazzles me,
the gazelle streaking whose hooves seem
to float over the ground, the stylish striping
of the zebra, a parade except against their
proper sun/shade pattern, the storm cloud
glory of horses, antelope's skin of velvet dust,
the calm guilt-provoking gaze of ruminants.

But I am neither. I honor my mothers,
scuttling mammals hustling through the brush
who gobbled through life, a little of this,
a little of that, a lot of what others left,
grasshoppers, a nice fat mouse, berries,
rotten apples to get drunk on, roots
we dug for, never efficiently. Not special-
ized to do anything particularly well.

Those middling animals, the small predators
like the feral cat always chasing dinner
and scrambling away from being eaten; the small
grey fox who picks grapes on the high dunes
and will steal a melon or a goose. Behold
my ancestral portraits: shambling field
apes smallish and chattering, with babies
hanging on their backs picking over the fruit
like my grandmother, my mother and like me.

The answer to all problems

We aren't available, we can't talk to you
right now, but you can talk to us, we say,
but think of the astonishment if machines
suddenly spoke truth: what do you want?

You'd best have a damned good reason for bothering
me, intruding on my silence. If you're bored,
read a good book. Masturbate on your own time.
Call weather or your mother or a talk show.

If you're a creditor, I've just been cremated.
If you're my ex, I'm fucking a perfect body
in Acapulco. Hi, I'm too shy to answer.
I'm scared of obscene calls. I'm paranoid.

I'm sharing a bottle of wine and a loaf of bread
with my lover, our flesh smokes with desire,
our lips brush, our clothes uncoil hissing,
and you have a problem? Try prayer.

Hi obtuse one, it may be eleven on the West Coast
but it's two a.m. here and as you listen
a pitch too high for you to hear is giving
you herpes and melting your elastic and Velcro.

Hi, this is the machine. My person is standing
two feet away to hear if you're worth the effort.
Hi. If you hang up without leaving a message
your teeth will loosen overnight.

Hi, can my machine call your machine
and make an appointment? Can my machine
mate with yours and breed iPods?
Hi, my humans have been murdered and cannot come.

After the corn moon

Swallows thrown from a giant hand turn,
fleet motes, around each other hurtling
over the marsh and back. The young
grown, the flock assembles. On the wire
neat, formal, they turn sleek heads south.

Every rambling poison ivy vine burns
in a few scarlet leaves. Grass tawny
as lions, the salt meadow has fur now
rippling over bunched muscles in the wind,
leaner and raspier than last week,

hungrier for something to rub, something
to strip. The robins are drunk on rum
cherries. The garlic falls over. The rose
hips redden. Every day we peer at the grapes
watching them color, puckering sour.

The houses are all rented and the roads
jammed with people driving their tempers
flat out or boiling their brains dry
in traffic like percolators searing
good coffee to battery acid.

Soon they will go home and the ponds
will clean themselves of soapsuds and the piss
of psychiatrists' children and the fried clam
shacks will put up their shutters and the air
will smell of salt and pine again.

This land is a room where a party has gone
on too long. Nothing is left whole to break.
As the blowzy embrace of heat slackens
I long for the feisty bite of cold mornings,
the bracing smack of the sea wind after

the first storm, walking the great beach alone.
The bed of summer needs changing to roughened
sheets that smell of the line. Fall seeps in
like energy quickening till it bursts out
spurting crimson from creeper and tree.

Even in this heat I walk farther and faster
hearing the sea's rising mutter. The birds
seem all in a hurry. The season of death
and fruition is nearly upon us. Sometimes
the knife of frost is a blessing.

77

Perfect weather

On the six o'clock news, Ken poses in his three
piece blue suit beside the map of fronts.
Barbie pretends to slap at him. "Now Ken,
I hope you aren't going to give us bad weather!"
"I'm giving you perfect 10 weather, Barbie,
not a cloud all weekend! Not a storm in sight
on our Super Weather Radar. Another
perfect week coming up." "Oh, thank you, Ken!"

Gods in the box, they pop out grinning.
Next will come the announcements of water
shortages on the South Shore, crop
failure in the Pioneer Valley, a fire raging
through the pitch pines near Sandwich.
Turn on the faucet, Barbie. Think that's
manufactured in some plant in Maine?
Shipped from Taiwan like your microphone?

It arrives in pellets called rain drops. That's
what you call bad and mean it: nasty weather.
They want a permanent pasted on sun
to shine over the freeze dried face and the body
resembling exactly a mannequin in a shop
window sipping an empty glass on Astroturf.
That body will never thicken or that face
admit it liked to smile or frown: wiped memory.

A permanent now called lobotomy
under a sunlamp sky, a neon moon, life as a golf
course unrolled from a truck and every day
you can play. Everyone you meet has just
your skin color and income level; the dys-
functional are removed immediately to storage.
Service personnel speak another language.
Death comes as a power failure.

Ken, how's supper? Did you know bluefish
swim? Kiwi grow on trees made of bad weather
juice? Perrier actually bubbles out of rock?
Under the carpet under the cracking cement
below the power lines and the toxic waste stored
in old mines is molten rock, the hot liquid heart
of the earth beating, about to erupt
blowing the clots out of its ancient veins.

We don't own the earth, not even the way
you buy a condo, Ken. We don't time-share
here, but live on it as hair grows
on the scalp, from inside; we are part
of earth, not visitors using the facilities.
If the plumbing breaks down, we can't move out
to a bigger house. Rain is earth's blood
and ours while we swim and life swims in us.

Pray for rain. Go out on the earth barefoot
and dance for rain. Take a small
ceremonial knife and slash your arms
so the thick red water inside trickles out.
Piss in the dust. Spit into the wind.
Go climb a mountain without a canteen to learn
how the swollen tongue sticks to the palate.
Then tell us what good weather you're providing.

Moon of the mother turtle

I am the busybody who interferes.
All through turtle mating season
I am hauling the females out of the road
and setting them where I presume
it is safe to lay their eggs.

Who appointed me guardian of turtles?
Yet when I see their bodies broken
like rotten pumpkins on the blacktop
I get so angry I have no choice but
to go on dragging them to sandbanks.

My least favorite duty is the two weeks
of snapping turtles. Occasionally I grasp
a weighty female and haul her out
of the way of cars before she can react.
Other times it's a wrestling match,

me with a stick and she with her beak,
neither of us prepared to back down,
a tug-of-war, wrestling, snarling
in the ruts of the old railroad right-of-way.
She must, she must. The eggs press

on her to be born. She is half mad.
Her eyes glitter dully as sun
glimpsed through muddy water. She is
an ancient ancestor raging with the urge
to dig and lay, dig and lay more.

I am a yelping dog circling, just as mad
to get her out of the roadway. She
hisses like a mother cat. Her great
beak clacks. She stinks like muck
from the basement of the fish maker's shop.

When finally I get her onto the bank, she
goes to it at once, sighing. A train
could pass two feet away as it used to
and she would lay on. I am forgotten
as I haul two ties to build her a rampart.

Then we go our separate ways, me toward
the bay to complete my four-mile walk,
she back to Bound Brook, dragging her
massive belly, each under our compulsions
like moons with the same and different faces.

Baboons in the perennial bed

Even after common sense whittles ambition
I always order too many seeds, bulbs, corms.
What's the lure? Why am I torn between
cutting the lily for my bedside and savoring
it daily on its pedestal of crisp leaves?

They rouse and sate the senses, touch,
sight, scent, the wild shagginess and precise
sculpted lines, the shadings of color from clang
to sigh. Yet I think what moves underneath
is pleased envy at their flagrancy.

They wave their sexual organs in the air,
the plants, colored far more freely than the hind-
quarters of baboons. We who are raised to shame
for the moist orchid between our thighs
must wish we were as certain of our beauty.

Something to look forward to

Menopause: word used as an insult,
a menopausal woman, mind or poem
as if not to leak regularly or on the caprice
of the moon, the collision of egg and sperm,
were the curse we first learned to call that blood.

I have twisted myself to praise that bright splash.
When my womb opens its lips on the full
or dark of the moon, that connection
aligns me as it does the sea. I quiver,
a compass needle thrilling with magnetism.

Yet for every celebration there's the time
it starts on a jet with the seatbelt sign on.
Consider the trail of red amoebae
crawling onto hostess' sheets to signal
my body's disregard of calendar, clock.

How often halfway up the side of a mountain,
during a demonstration with the tactical police
force drawn up in tanks between me and a toilet;
during an endless wind machine panel with four males
I the token woman and they with iron bladders,

I have felt that wetness and wanted to strangle
my womb like a mouse. Sometimes it feels cosmic
and sometimes it feels like mud. Yes, I have prayed
to my blood on my knees in toilet stalls
simply to show its rainbow of deliverance.

My friend Penny at twelve, being handed a napkin
the size of an ironing board cover, cried out
I have to do this from now till I die?
No, said her mother, it stops in middle age.
Good, said Penny, there's something to look forward to.

Today supine, groaning with demon crab claws
gouging my belly, I tell you I will secretly dance
and pour out a cup of wine on the earth
when time stops that leak permanently;
I will burn my last tampons as votive candles.

Litter

I am always forgetting something.
The kettle boils dry and stinks.
The tiny green-shouldered tomato plants
while I'm writing a poem die of thirst
scorched under the glass of the hotbed.

I forget birthdays, I forget to call.
I forget the book I promised to bring.
I forget where I put my purse, my keys,
my wallet, my lenses, my love.
I lose my way in night's black pocket.

I can't think of the name of the goddess
who stands at the gate blinking her one
great eye through the fog and the snarling
wind, sweeping her warning glance across
where the waves smash themselves kneeling.

I forget the way my mother laughed.
I forget her cake, the taste of the uncooked
dough, the just proportions of cinnamon and sugar.
I lose the touch of her fingers, stone
washed smooth by water and laid in the sun.

I lose the bread smell of my old cat's fur;
I lose the name and face of a man just out
of prison who crawled in my body to hide;
I lose the addresses of urgent people to whom
I promised much in towns I have forgotten.

What happened to my burnt orange shawl?
My bones are slowly dissolving in salt water.
It all falls away like feathers, like leaves,
like sand blowing. In the end I will say,
I was somebody maybe a woman I forget.

All the lost words and things and tasks
I have littered behind me are drifting on winds
round and up as if gravity had forgotten
to drop them, and sometimes in the night
I wake and the name comes to me and I shout

to the ceiling, Appomattox, rue de Sentier,
Emily Hannah, 8325 American Avenue,
metasomatism, two thirds to one,
and then lilacs, the scent of my mother's
white lilacs, thickens the air till I weep.

The bottom line

That white withered angel cancer
steals into a house through cracks,
lurks in the foundation, the walls,
litters down its infinitesimal dandruff
from school ceilings into children's lungs.

That invisible fungus hides in processed food,
in the cereal, the salami, the cake.
Welcomed into the body like a friend
it proceeds to eat you from inside,
parasitic wasp in a tomato worm.

Out of what caprice quenched in a moment's
pleasure does the poison seep?
We come to mistrust the body
a slave to be starved to submission,
an other that can like a rabid dog

turn on and bite a separate me.
But the galloping horse of the thighs,
the giraffe of the spine are innocent
browsing their green. We die of decisions
made at 3:15 in boardrooms.

We die of the bottom line. We die
of stockholders' dividends and a big bonus
for top executives and more perks. Cancer
is the white radioactive shadow of profit
falling across, withering the dumb flesh.

Morning love song

I am filled with love like a melon
with seeds, I am ripe and dripping sweet juices.
If you knock gently on my belly
it will thrum ripe, ripe.

It is high green summer with the strawberries
just ending and the blueberries coloring,
with the roses tumbling like fat Persian
kittens, the gold horns of the squash blowing.

The day after a storm the leaves gleam.
The world is clear as a just washed picture window.
The air whips its fine silk through the hands.
Every last bird has an idea to insist on.

I am trying to work and instead
I drip love for you like a honeycomb.
I am devoid of fantasies clean as rainwater
waiting to flow all over your skin.

Implications of one plus one

Sometimes we collide, tectonic plates merging,
continents shoving, crumpling down into the molten
veins of fire deep in the earth and raising
tons of rock into jagged crests of Sierra.

Sometimes your hands drift on me, milkweed's
airy silk, wingtip's feathery caresses,
our lips grazing, a drift of desires gathering
like fog over warm water, thickening to rain.

Sometimes we go to it heartily, digging,
burrowing, grunting, tossing up covers
like loose earth, nosing into the other's
flesh with hot nozzles and wallowing there.

Sometimes we are kids making out, silly
in the quilt, tickling the xylophone spine,
blowing wet jokes, loud as a whole
slumber party bouncing till the bed breaks.

I go round and round you sometimes, scouting,
blundering, seeking a way in, the high boxwood
maze I penetrate running lungs bursting
toward the fountain of green fire at the heart.

Sometimes you open wide as cathedral doors
and yank me inside. Sometimes you slither
into me like a snake into its burrow.
Sometimes you march in with a brass band.

Ten years of fitting our bodies together
and still they sing wild songs in new keys.
It is more and less than love: timing,
chemistry, magic and will and luck.

One plus one equals one, unknowable except
in the moment, not convertible into words,
not explicable or philosophically interesting.
But it is. And it is. And it is. Amein.

Sun-day poacher

My uncle Zimmy worked the face down in the soft
coal mines that hollowed out the long ridged
mountains of Pennsylvania, where the enamel
under the spigot in the claw tub at home
was stained the color of rust from iron.

In the winter he went down before the sun
came up, and when he rose, it had sunk,
a world of darkness down in the damp,
then up in the cold where the stars burned
like the sparks you see on squinted eyes.

On Sunday he hunted, gliding over the bristly
ridges that hid the tunnels, hollow rocks
whose blasted faces were bearded by shining ice.
That was his way to the sun blessing his eyes
and the tingling air the pines electrified.

He could only go with a rifle on his shoulder.
Men couldn't just walk and look. He had
to be doing something. With tenderness he sighted
the deer and shot true, disemboweled on the spot,
the snow marked with a widening rose of blood.

He butchered there and brought home venison,
better than the wan meat of the company store.
Nothing but bones would mark the spot in three
days. In winter, every bird and beast burns
with hunger, eats or snuffs out with cold.

He walked on top of the mountains he mined within
where and how he pleased, quiet as the snow
to kill. My aunt Margaret fell in love

with him and her father mocked and threatened.
A schoolteacher marry a miner? She did, fast.

You could see the way he touched her the power
they kindled between them. It was a dance
at Monday's Corner. He roared home on the icy
roads with the whiskey stoking that furnace hot.
That was how men drove: fast and often drunk.

He loved her still the year she lingered on.
Money could have saved her, of course.
A child, I ate his venison adoring him,
the strength and speed of a great black bear,
the same fatality in his embrace.

Burial by salt

The day after Thanksgiving I took you to the sea.
The sky was low and scudding. The wind was stiff.
The sea broke over itself in seething froth
like whipped up eggwhites, blowing to settle
in slowly popping masses at my feet.

I ran, boots on, into the bucking surf
taking you in handfuls, tossing you
into wind, into water, into the elements:
go back, give back. Time is all spent,
the flesh is spent to ashes.

Mother's were colored like a mosaic,
vivid hues of the inside of conch shells,
pastels, pearls, green, salmon as feathers
of tropical birds. They fit in my cupped hands.
I put her in the rose garden and said Kaddish.

Your ashes are old movies, black into grey.
Heavy as iron filings, they sag the box
sides. They fill it to overflowing.
Handful after handful I give to the waves
which seize and churn you over and under.

I am silent as I give you to the cold
winter ocean grey as a ship of war,
the color of your eyes, grey with green
and blue washed in, that so seldom met
my gaze, that looked right through me.

What is to be said? Did you have a religion?
If so, you never spoke of it to me.
I remember your saying No, saying it often
and loud, I remember your saying, Never,
I remember, I won't have that in my house.

I grew up under the threat of your anger
as peasants occupy the slopes of a volcano
sniffing the wind, repeating old adages,
reading birdflight and always waiting, even
in sleep for the ground to quake and open.

My injustices, my pains, my resentments;
they are numerous, precious as the marbles
I kept in a jar, not so much for playing
as simply rolling in my hands to see
the colors trap the light and swell.

Tossing your ashes in my hands as the waves
drag the sand from under me, trying to topple
me into the turning eddy of far storms,
I want to cast that anger from me, finally
to say, you begot me and although my body

my hair, my eyes are my mother's so that at your
funeral, your brother called me by her name,
I will agree that in the long bones of my legs,
in my knees, in my Welsh mouth that sits oddly
in my Jewish Tartar face, you are imprinted.

I was born the wrong sex to a woman
in her mid-forties who had tried to get pregnant
for five years. A hard birth,
I was her miracle and your disappointment.
Everything followed from that, downhill.

I search now through the ashes of my old pain
to find something to praise, and I find that
withholding love, you made me strive to be worthy,
reaching, always reaching, thinking that when I leaped
high enough you would be watching. You weren't.

That did not cancel the leaping or the fruit
at last grasped in the hand and gnawed to the pit.
You were the stone on which I built my strength.
Your indifference honed me. Your coldness
toughened my flesh. You anger stropped me.

I was reading maps for family trips at age
five, navigating from the backseat. Till
I was twenty, I did not know other children
did not direct all turns and plot route numbers.
When Mother feigned helplessness, I was factotum.

Nurse, houseboy, carpenter's helper, maid,
whatever chinks appeared I filled, responsible
and rebellious with equal passion, equal time,
and thus quite primed to charge like a rocket
out the door trailing sparks at seventeen.

We were illsuited as fox and bull. Once
I stopped following baseball, we could not talk.
I'd ask you how some process was done—open
hearth steel, how generators worked.
Your answers had a clarity I savored.

I did with Mother as I had promised her,
I took her from you and brought her home to me,
I buried her as a Jew and mourn her still.
To you I made no promises. You asked none.
Forty-nine years we spoke of nothing real.

For decades I thought someday we would talk
at last. In California I came to you in the mountains
at the dam carrying that fantasy like a picnic
lunch beautifully cooked and packed, but never
to be eaten. Not by you and me.

When I think of the rare good times
I am ten or eleven and we are working together
on some task in silence. In silence I faded into
the cartoon son. Hand me the chisel. I handed.
Bevel the edge smooth. I always got bored.

I'd start asking questions, I'd start asking
why and wherefore and how come and who said so.
I was lonely on the icefield, I was lonely
in the ice caves of your sometime favor.
I kept trying to start a fire or conversation.

Time burns down and the dark rushes in in waves.
I can't lie. What was between us was history,
not love. I have striven to be just to you,
stranger, first cause, old man, my father,
and now I give you over to salt and silence.

Eat fruit

Keep your legs crossed, Mother said. Drinking
leads to babies. Don't hang around street corners.
I rushed to gulp moonshine on corners, hip outthrust.
So why in the butter of my brain does one marble tablet
shine bearing my mother's commandment, eat fruit?

Here I stand, the only poet from whom
you can confidently obtain after a reading
enough mushy tan bananas to bake bread
should you happen to feel the urge at ten
some night in East Lansing or Boise.

Others litter ash, beer cans. I leak pits.
As we descend into Halifax while my seat partner
is snorting the last of his coke, I am the one
choking as I gobble three apples in five minutes,
agricultural contraband seized at borders.

Customs agents throw open my suitcase and draw
out with gingerly leer from under my negligee
a melon. Drug smugglers feed their self-importance,
but me they hate along with the guy trying to smuggle
in a salami from the old country his uncle gave him.

I am the slob who makes gory stains on railroad seats
with fermenting strawberries. You can recognize me
by the happy cloud of winged creatures following my head.
I have raised more fruitflies than genetics labs.
I have endowed ant orphanages and retirement communities.

However, I tell you smugly, I am regular in Nome,
in Paducah, in both Portlands and all Springfields.
While you are eating McMuffins I am savoring a bruised
but extremely sophisticated pear that has seen five
airports and four cities and grown old in wisdom.

Dead Waters

At Aigues Mortes the dog was a practiced beggar.
He patrolled not the big lot where buses disgorge
but a small seaward lot near the private quarter.

We ate our picnic lunch, gazing at the ramparts.
He honed his longing stare on us till we tossed
bits of sausage he caught deftly and bolted.

Finally we threw him a baguette, whole and slightly
stale, thinking he would leave it, teasing him.
But his ears rose as if he heard a fine clear

high note our ears could not reach. He caught the loaf.
He laid it down to examine and then he seized it,
tossed his head smartly and set off at a rapid trot,

the prized baguette in his teeth. Other picnickers called
to him, we tossed after him a bit of sausage, but
he could not be lured back. Off he went in a straight

line at the ramparts and then all along them
to the far gate when he headed in and ran home,
never pausing under the white fish eye of the sun.

A whole loaf of bread. What did that mean to him?
The thing humans never give him? Therefore precious?
Or simply something entire, seamless, perfect for once.

The housing project at Drancy

Trains without signs flee through Paris.
Wrong trains. The wrong station.
The world as microwave oven, burning from within.
We arrive. Drancy looks like Inkster,
Gary, the farther reaches of Newark.

In the station they won't give directions.
C'est pas notre affaire. We don't deal with that.
Outside five buses limp in five directions
into the hot plain drugged with exhaust.
Nobody ever heard of the camp. They turn away.

Out on the bridge, over marshaling yards:
here Jews were stuffed into cars nailed shut.
Here children too young to know their names
were counted like so many shoes
as they begged the French police hemming them in,

Take me to the bathroom, please, please,
before I wet myself. Mother, I have been so good,
and it is so very dark. Dear concierge,
I am writing to you as everyone else
is dead now and they are taking me away.

Yes, to the land children named Pitchepois,
giant's skull land grimmer than Hansel came to.
On the bridge I saw an old bald workman
staring down and I told myself desperately,
He is a Communist and will answer me.

I asked him where the camp was, now a housing
project. He asked, Why do you want to know?
I had that one ready. No talk of novels, research.
My aunt was there. Oh, in that case,
he pointed to distant towers. You want that bus.

Where we descended the bus, Never heard of it.
Eyes that won't look. Then a woman asked that
same question, Why do you want to know?
A housing project crammed with mothers.
The guard towers are torn down and lindens grow.

In flats now with heat and plumbing, not eighty
but one family lives. Pain still rises,
the groaning of machinery deep underfoot.
Crimes ignored sink into the soil like PCBs
and enter the bones of children.

Black Mountain

On Montagne Noire creeping everywhere under the beech trees
were immense black slugs the size and pattern
of blown truck tires exploded by the superhighway.
Diamonds patterned their glossy and glittering backs.

As we watched, leaves, whole flowers disappeared in three bites.
Such avidity rebuked our stomachs skittish with alien
water and strange food. In patches of sunlight filtered
down, the slugs shone like wet black glass.

Battlefields are like any other fields; a forest
where men and women fought tanks with sten guns
houses as many owl and rabbit and deer as the next hill
where nothing's happened since the Romans passed by.

Yet I have come without hesitation through the maze
of lumbering roads to this spot where the small marker
tells us we have reached a destination. To die here
under hemlock's dark drooping boughs, better I think

than shoved into the showers of gas to croak like roaches
too packed in to flail in the intense slow pain
as the minutes like lava cooling petrified the jammed
bodies into living rock, basalt pillars whose fingers

gouged grooves in cement. Yes, better to drop in the high
clean air and let your blood soak into the rich leaf mold.
Better to get off one good shot. Better to remember trains
derailed, turntables wrecked with plastique, raids

on the munitions dump. Better to die with a gun
in your hand you chose to pick up and had time to shoot.
Dying you pass out of choice. The others come, put up
a monument decorated with crosses, no Mogen Davids.

I come avid and omnivorous as the shining slugs.
I have eaten your history and made it myth;
among the tall trees of your pain my characters walk.
A saw whines in the valley. I say Kaddish for you.

Blessed only is the act. The act of defiance,
the act of justice that fills the mouth with blood.
Blessed is the act of survival that saves the blood.
Blessed is the act of art that paints the blood

redder than real and quicker, that restores
the fallen tree to its height and birds. Memory
is the simplest form of prayer. Today you glow
like warm precious lumps of amber in my mind.

The ram's horn sounding

Giant porcupine, I walk a rope braided
of my intestines and veins, beige and blue and red,
while clutched in my arms, you lie glaring
sore eyed, snuffling and sticking your spines at me.

Always I am finding quills worked into some unsuspected
muscle, an innocent pillow of fat pierced by you.
We sleep in the same bed nightly and you take it all.
I wake shuddering with cold, the quilt stripped from me.

No, not a porcupine: a leopard cub.
Beautiful you are as light and as darkness.
Avid, fierce, demanding with sharp teeth
to be fed and tended, you only want my life.

Ancient, living, a deep and tortuous river
that rose in the stark mountains beyond the desert,
you have gouged through rocks with slow persistence
enduring, meandering in long shining coils to the sea.

2.

A friend who had been close before being recruited
by the CIA once sent me a postcard of the ghetto at Tetuan
yellowed like old pornography numbered 17,
a prime number as one might say a prime suspect.

The photographer stood well clear of the gate
to shoot old clothes tottering in the tight street,
beards matted and holy with grease,
children crooked under water jugs,
old men austere and busy as hornets.
Flies swarmed on the lens.
Dirt was the color.

Oh, I understood your challenge.
My Jewishness seemed to you sentimental,
perverse, planned obsolescence.
Paris was hot and dirty the night I first
met relatives who had survived the war.
My identity squatted whining on my arm

gorging itself on my thin blood.
A gaggle of fierce insistent speakers of ten
languages had different passports mother
from son, brother from sister, had four
passports all forged, kept passports
from gone countries (Transylvania, Bohemia,
old despotisms fading like Victorian wallpaper),
were used to sewing contraband into coat
linings. I smuggled for them across two borders.
Their wars were old ones.
Mine was just starting.

Old debater, it's easy in any manscape
to tell the haves from the have-nots.
Any ghetto is a Klein bottle.
You think you are outside gazing idly in.
Winners write history; losers
die of it, like the plague.

3.

A woman and a Jew, sometimes more
of a contradiction than I can sweat out,
yet finally the intersection that is both
collision and fusion, stone and seed.

Like any poet I wrestle the holy name
and know there is no wording finally
can map, constrain or summon that fierce
voice whose long wind lifts my hair

chills my skin and fills my lungs
to bursting. I serve the word
I cannot name, who names me daily,
who speaks me out by whispers and shouts.

Coming to the new year, I am picked
up like the ancient ram's horn to sound

over the congregation of people and beetles,
of pines, whales, marshhawks and asters.

Then I am dropped into the factory of words
to turn my little wheels and grind my own
edges, back on piecework again, knowing
there is no justice we don't make daily

like bread and love. Shekinah,
stooping on hawk wings prying into my heart
with your silver beak; floating down
a milkweed silk dove of sunset;

riding the filmy sheets of rain like a ghost
ship with all sails still unfurled;
bless me and use me for telling and naming
the forever collapsing shades and shapes of life,

the rainbows cast across our eyes by the moment
of sun, the shadows we trail across the grass
running, the opal valleys of the night flesh,
the moments of knowledge ripping into the brain

and aligning everything into a new pattern
as a constellation learned organizes blur
into stars, the blood kinship with all green, hairy
and scaled folk born from the ancient warm sea.

from
Mars and Her Children

The ark of consequence

The classic rainbow shows as an arc,
a bridge strung in thinning clouds,
but I have seen it flash a perfect circle,
rising and falling and rising again
through the octave of colors,
a sun shape rolling like a wheel of light.

Commonly it is a fraction of a circle,
a promise only partial, not a banal
sign of safety like a smile pin,
that rainbow cartoon affixed to vans
and baby carriages. No, it promises
only, this world will not self-destruct.

Account the rainbow a boomerang of liquid
light, foretelling rather that what we
toss out returns in the water table;
flows from the faucet into our bones;
what we shoot up into orbit falls
to earth through the roof one night.

Think of it as a promise that what
we do continues in an arc
of consequence, flickers in our
children's genes, collects in each
spine and liver, gleams in the apple,
coats the down of the drowning auk.

When you see the rainbow iridescence
shiver in the oil slick, smeared
on the waves of the poisoned river,
shudder for the covenant broken, for we
are given only this floating round ark
with the dead moon for company and warning.

The ex in the supermarket

I see him among the breakfast foods
reading labels with a dissatisfied air.
He looks softened, blurred, as if his body
had been left underwater too long.

I reach for that old pain and find it
discrete, anonymous, mildly bitter
as aspirin. It dissolves in my blood
as I try to taste it, leaving a chemical burn.

The first severed year, I avoided him
like an open pit of acid that could peel
the flesh from the skeleton of my pain.
Each bone would squeal, disjointed, red.

Now I could walk through him like smoke
and only sneeze. The pain has dispersed
into its atoms. Yet in each tiny ball
is encoded immense violent energy.

Memory explodes of itself, cracked by a scent
of mayflower, of hot rubber, of cumin.
The past ignites in banal words of a pop song,
burning the walls of the present into gas.

I cannot walk the dog of the past at my
convenience. When memory howls gnashing
at the rusty moon, it does not even sniff at
that man pondering the peanut butter of his choice.

Your eyes recall old fantasies

The Aegean of your eyes—remembered
spring of thirty years ago
when you were an abused, drugged child
and I dragged through Greek villages
with a man who daily polished his anger
till it shone whitely as glass
in the sun, kept it hidden,
denied, until he buried
its dagger in my flesh.

The landscape loved me instead.
The poppies shouted orgasm.
The light brushed my bones
till they glowed secretly,
cuneiform shapes in the night
of my despair, an alphabet
beginning to form that when
I returned would shape
poems in my changing voice.

That sea was clear down to dark
sharp rocks, the shapes of ancient
wrecks; teemed with dancing octopi,
red mullet flashing like glimpses
of desire teasing me with hope.
Then the wind roused it to opaque
fury, thudding like granite
against the prow of the boat
that bore a woman's staring eye.

It was the eye of the bold
sensual woman of the Cretan wall
paintings who walked bare breasted
without fear across the goddess's
rocky lap. Your joy is too young
for you, the oracle murmured,
but I was too young to understand,
promises etched in my flesh
in a language I could not yet read.

Getting it back

When the guests have gone, the house is twice
as big. Quiet blows through it like silver
light that touches every chair and plate
to the precision of objects in a Vermeer.

We face each other and slowly begin to talk,
not making conversation as one plans and then
cooks a company dinner, but improvising,
the words spiraling up and out in a dance

as intricate and instinctual as the choral
wave of swallows darting on the silken
twilight pale as a moon snail shell, till between
us the hanging nest of our intimacy is rewoven.

How the full moon wakes you

The white cat is curled up in the sky
its cloudy tail drawn round its flanks.
Waking, it struts over the roofs singing
down chimneys, its claws clicking

on the roof tiles that loosen and fall.
Now it runs along the bare boughs of the oak.
Now it leaps to the beech and sharpens
its long yellow claws. Sparks fly out.

The moon is hungry and calls to be fed,
cries to come into the bedroom through
the skylight and crawl under the covers,
to curl up at your breast and purr.

The moon caterwauls on the back fence
saying I burn, I am hot as molten silver.
I am the dancer on the roof who wakes you.
Rise to me and I will melt you to silk dust.

I am the passion you have forgotten
in your long sleep, but now your bones glow
through your flesh, your eyes see in the dark.
On owl wings you will hunt through the night.

The cat's song

Mine, says the cat, putting out his paw of darkness.
My lover, my friend, my slave, my toy, says
the cat making on your chest his gesture of drawing
milk from his mother's forgotten breasts.

Let us walk in the woods, says the cat.
I'll teach you to read the tabloid of scents,
to fade into shadow, wait like a trap, to hunt.
Now I lay this plump warm mouse on your mat.

You feed me, I try to feed you, we are friends,
says the cat, although I am superior to you.
Can you leap twenty times the height of your body?
Can you run up and down trees? Jump between roofs?

Let us rub our bodies together and talk of touch.
My emotions are pure as salt crystals and as hard.
My lusts glow like my eyes. I sing to you in the mornings
walking round and round your bed and into your face.

Come I will teach you to dance as naturally
as falling asleep and waking and stretching long, long.
I speak greed with my paws and fear with my whiskers.
Envy lashes my tail. Love speaks me entire, a word

of fur. I will teach you to be still as an egg
and to slip like the ghost of wind through the grass.

The hunger moon

The snow is frozen moonlight on the marshes.
How bright it is tonight, the air thin
as a skim of black ice and serrated,
cutting the lungs. My eyes sting.

Spring, I watch the moon for instruction
in planting; summer, I gauge her grasp
on the tides of the sea, the bay, my womb:
now you may gather oysters, now lay

the white, the red, the black beans
into the earth eyes rolled upwards.
But winters, we are in opposition.
I must fight the strong pulls of the body.

The blood croons, curl to sleep, embryo in a seed.
Early to sleep, late to rise from the down cave.
Even at seven night still squats in the pines.
Swim in the womb of dreams and grow new limbs.

Awake at last, the body begins to crave,
not salads, not crisp apples and sweet kiwis,
but haunches of beef and thick fatty stews.
Eat, whispers the crone in the bone, eat.

The hunger moon is grinning like a skull.
The bats are asleep. The little voles
streak starving through tunnels in the snow
and voracious shrews race after them.

Eat, make fat against famine, grow round
while there's something rich to gnaw on,
urges the crone from her peasant wisdom.
She wants every woman her own pumpkin,

she wants me full as tonight's moon
when I long to wane. Why must I fight her,
who taught my mother's mother's mothers
to survive the death marches of winters past?

For Mars and her children returning in March

Mars is the name of a female humpback whale

1.

To name is not to possess what cannot
be owned or even known in the small words
and endless excuses of human speech.
I have adopted a humpback whale, Mars.

When I renew my support for whale research
a photo comes, usually her flukes—
diving or perhaps slapping the water.
Fictional bond, sucker bait, gimmick.

Last winter while humpbacks
were washing up week by week, she birthed,
the year of heaviness issuing in life,
her sisters about her attending.

So every spring I wait to see if she
returns, for naming makes valuable to us
what is unique in itself, one of four hundred
thirty-five local humpbacks we haven't yet killed.

2.

Jonah in the dark hears the immense heart throbbing
like a generator. Tours the cathedral of the lungs.
But now above the sloshing and churning,
the engine of the heart, he hears the voice of the whale.
He is inside the organ; the lungs are its bellows.

Its pipes are fathoms tall. He is a mouse hiding there.
He is carried inside a tenor the size of a concert hall
improvising on themes he hears now from all sides,
clicks, squeaks, moans, trills, it sounds electronic.
In the night the tones flicker and shimmer,

nets of sound trailing through the silence
constellations floating in the salty dark.
Our prayers rise like clouds of whining mosquitoes
give me, I want, I need, I must have him,
her, the heart of my enemy,

a mountain to strip-mine,
whales to harvest, while they sing
a dwindling psalm to the great eye that watches.

3.

Arcing out of the grey green moil of water
the humpback offers her plume of praise,
steam gusting from the hot stove of her heart.

They are houses leaping,
they are ore boats upending.
Lava flows, they float on the calm.
Leather icebergs, they are sunning in the current.

Breaching, now they travel in bow curves,
viaducts, strong arches of speed,
huge smooth wheels turning past us.

Now she rises just beside the boat,
thrusting herself out, dark joy towering
over me where I grip the slippery wet rail.
Her steam touches my face.

Her breath enters my nose and my lungs.
That small vulnerable eye bright like a chip
of obsidian looks at me, pale—staring in awe.

4.

Here on this question mark of sand sprawled
gracefully on the tumbling sea,
we know the whales one by one.
A dead warbler under the leafless bayberry
may provoke us to pass by with the flash
of mourning that flesh shudders out its breath
and turns cold, fading feathers in the brown
grasses dying back. But a dead whale:
a shrieking gyre of hungry seagulls turns
and turns over the heap of it, the eye
still open and not yet picked out.
Soon it stinks like a battlefield.
The bulldozer arrives to labor at burial.

We see the little as cute, the big as impressive
although we are oftener killed by viruses
than by an elephant in must.
But here the loss is not impersonal.
Each is known. Beltane, Comet, Point,
Talon noted among Cape friends dead this cycle.

We must praise each humpback breaching,
each a poet, a composer, a scholar of the roads
below. They are always singing, and what they know
is as alien to us as if they swam past Sirius.

Naming turns the crowd into faces,
turns no-man's-land into someone's turf,
making a stray and starving cat a pet.
Naming makes a whale who swims through the sea
strewn with human waste and poison,
the trash of boats and cities,
the nets and shipping, known to us,
pod and matrilineal descent, travels
and fate. One community encompasses
this fragile fawn-colored coil of sand
and the vast and roiling Gulf Stream river
and all finny, furred and feathered who dwell therein.

If we cannot preserve the greatest of these
then we will surely follow that shape of natural power
into the silence after its murdered song,
the sea lapping like heavy oil at beaches
where plastic shards cast up on the stained sand.

Sexual selection among birds

The soft breasted dun bird on her nest
incubating a clutch of sand colored eggs,
her dreams are scarlet and cobalt.

Her mate is gaudy, enameled like
a Fabergé egg, jeweled and singing:
the artifact of her aesthetic lust.

Over the bower of bush where she waits
he dances in the air, mine, mine:
but she knows better.

Of all the females, she, feathered
dinosaur, is the choosiest, the most
critical, demanding of her mate

not only fidelity, passion, offspring
but that he sing like Mozart
and bloom like a perfect rose.

Shad blow

Deer tracks cloven dark in the pale sand.
The grey squirrels shriek and chase each other
crashing from branch to branch of the oaks.

The shad bloom is late this year and perfect,
trees that are one great composite flower,
wild carrots, Queen Anne's lace the size

of giraffes riffled by the breeze
miles of salt have scrubbed
bone white. Orange and lemon orioles

flit among knotted branches. The trunks
of shad are grey, blotched with lichen,
fog caught and woven into wood.

2.

I used to lie under the sour cherry in the narrow
yard of the house where we moved the year
I turned fifteen. White galaxies that would become

wine by summer's end, pies in the sky,
flashed against the sulfurous clouds of Detroit—
blossoms out of mahogany bark shining.

Who will I be? The will to love
ate holes in my mind. I was riddled
like a sieve with sharp sour desires.

I can taste that raw homemade wine,
taste a sweet and sour intoxicating pain
so empty, wanting played shrilly on me

like the wind over the mouth of a bottle
compelling a keening too high pitched
for a human to notice, but the dog next

door flung back his head and howled too
and my cat came stepping through the unmown
grass to circle three times, then marked

the tree with his spray as I burned
to mark the world with something of mine.
Spring came on like cramps in a growing body.

3.

In spring I raise my head to sniff at scents.
I want to be out by the river watching the ale
wives straddling the current, humping upstream.

I thrust my hands into the cool rich soil,
the moss like fur between cracks of the bricks.
I want to roll like a big dog and shake free.

The salamander cool as jelly, darkly colored
as cabernet sauvignon lies on my palm
then leaps to freedom, snap, in the woodpile.

Appetite licks at the air, the tiny leaves
opening their clenched silken banners.
At two in the afternoon the fox runs on the beach

going to paw at the late alewives crossing
the bar where the brook eases into the bay.
A gull runs at him, then flaps off.

Once I thought the seasons were mine,
moods, passions, itches I could scratch,
voids I could fill with other's bodies.

Now I know I am in the seasons, of them.
The sun warms the upturned soil and my arm.
Spring moves through me like an armada of light.

Report of the 14th Subcommittee
on Convening a Discussion Group

This is how things begin to tilt into change,
how coalitions are knit from strands of hair,
of barbed wire, twine, knitting wool and gut,
how people ease into action arguing each inch,
but the tedium of it is watching granite erode.

Let us meet to debate meeting, the day, the time,
the length. Let us discuss whether we will sit
or stand or hang from the ceiling or take it lying
down. Let us argue about the chair and the table and
the chairperson and the motion to table the chair.

In the room fog gathers under the ceiling and thickens
in every brain. Let us form committees spawning
subcommittees all laying little moldy eggs of reports.
Under the grey fluorescent sun they will crack
to hatch scuttling lizards of more committees.

The Pliocene gathers momentum and fades.
The earth tilts on its axis. More and more snows
fall each winter and less melt each spring.
A new ice age is pressing the glaciers forward
over the floor. We watch the wall of ice advance.

We are evolving into molluscs, barnacles
clinging to wood and plastic, metal and smoke
while the stale and flotsam-laden tide of rhetoric
inches up the shingles and dawdles back.
This is true virtue: to sit here and stay awake,

to listen, to argue, to wade on through the muck
wrestling to some momentary small agreement
like a pinhead pearl prized from a dragon-oyster.
I believe in this democracy as I believe
there is blood in my veins, but oh, oh, in me

lurks a tyrant with a double-bladed ax who longs
to swing it wide and shining, who longs to stand
and shriek, You Shall Do as I Say, pig-bastards.
No more committees but only picnics and orgies
and dances. I have spoken. So be it forevermore.

True romance

In a room with a nylon carpet and a daybed
a woman is dancing with her eyes on the TV set.
The face of the singer gluts. For her
he is singing, this face more familiar
than any lover's, this man she has carried
wrapped like a chocolate in the crisp paper
of her heart since she was fifteen.

She loves him, she loves him, for him
she dances, thrusting her hips, arms reaching,
churning her mons at his face bigger than
the face of her husband and closer,
more real than the smell of her own sweat.

O sunbright hero whose strut is paid for
by Japanese cars, by computers, by lite beer.
O lithe bodies the camera fills with buttercream
of wishes, bodies thin and flawless as blank paper,
bodies with nipples and navels taped, bodies
on which the clothes are glued, faces coated
with polyurethane, how many men paw at their
wives' flesh trying to unearth your vinyl.

Things move fast in that bright world. A man
sees a woman across a room and she smiles
only at him. After a diet soda commercial,
she is in bed with him. In the next scene
she is gone and his buddy the talking dog
goes at his side. Then the cars chase each other
off cliffs into balls of flame. The hero
steps out with a grin promising he will unzip
you, walk into the set of your head, turn up
the brightness and volume control till you
become real too, as the box glued to your eyes.

Woman in the bushes

A snail easing gingerly
tasting the morning's dangers with soft
gelatinous eyestalks probing
she shuffles forward, her only house
her back bearing all her clothes
and her shopping cart piled with
blanket roll, her Sterno, pan and bottle,
her photographs wilted like flowers.

This fall she sleeps in a rhodo-
dendron thicket in the park,
withdrawing deep among the leathery
leaves when twilight makes of grass
a minefield of exploding boys.

While the joggers prance past,
the cyclists in neon gear,
she wriggles out, washes
at a fountain, fills her bottle.
In the hollow among oaks shedding
she squats where the police
cannot see and heats beans.

Nothing human separates
us like comfort.
A local doctor describes a body dead
of exposure last winter: multiparous,
more than one child delivered.
Her teeth revealed a life once affluent.

Hunger sucked her like a spider.
We despise what isn't new. We toss
half of what we buy. Things are made
to break and we discard them. Excess
people take longer to get rid of
but they biodegrade nicely.
It just takes time and weather.

Apple sauce for Eve

Those old daddies cursed you and us in you,
damned for your curiosity: for your sin
was wanting knowledge. To try, to taste,
to take into the body, into the brain
and turn each thing, each sign, each factoid
round and round as new facets glint and white
fractures into colors and the image breaks
into crystal fragments that pierce the nerves
while the brain casts the chips into patterns.

Each experiment sticks a finger deep in the pie,
dares existence, blows a horn in the ear
of belief, lets the nasty and difficult brats
of real questions into the still air
of the desiccated parlor of stasis.
What we all know to be true, constant,
melts like frost landscapes on a window
in a jet of steam. How many last words
in how many dead languages would translate into,
But what happens if I, and Whoops!

We see Adam wagging his tail, good dog, good
dog, while you and the snake shimmy up the tree,
lab partners in a dance of will and hunger,
that thirst not of the flesh but of the brain.
Men always think women are wanting sex,
cock, snake, when it is the world she's after.
Then birth trauma for the first conceived kid
of the ego, I think therefore I am, I
kick the tree, who am I, why am I,
going, going to die, die, die.

You are indeed the mother of invention,
the first scientist. Your name means
life: finite, dynamic, swimming against
the current of time, tasting, testing,
eating knowledge like any other nutrient.
We are all the children of your bright hunger.
We are all products of that first experiment,
for if death was the worm in that apple,
the seeds were freedom and the flowering of choice.

The Book of Ruth and Naomi

When you pick up the Tanakh and read
the Book of Ruth, it is a shock
how little it resembles memory.
It's concerned with inheritance,
lands, men's names, how women
must wiggle and wobble to live.

Yet women have kept it dear
for the beloved elder who
cherished Ruth, more friend than
daughter. Daughters leave. Ruth
brought even the baby she made
with Boaz home as a gift.

Where you go, I will go too,
your people shall be my people,
I will be a Jew for you,
for what is yours I will love
as I love you, oh Naomi
my mother, my sister, my heart.

Show me a woman who does not dream
a double, heart's twin, a sister
of the mind in whose ear she can whisper,
whose hair she can braid as her life
twists its pleasure and pain and shame.
Show me a woman who does not hide

in the locket of bone that deep
eye beam of fiercely gentle love
she had once from mother, daughter,
sister; once like a warm moon
that radiance aligned the tides
of her blood into potent order.

At the season of first fruits we remember
those travelers, coconspirators, scavengers
making do with leftovers and mill ends,
whose friendship was stronger than fear,
stronger than hunger, who walked together
down death's dusty road, hands joined.

Of the patience called forth by transition

Notice how the sky is a milky opal
cloudless from rim to rim, of an indefinite
height and sliding now at midafternoon
into darkness. Pearly, it melts
imperceptibly into yellow and green,
willow colors from another season,
or the yellow of aspen leaves already fallen,
into lavender now, the sea lavender
shriveled in the marshes. As the trees
reduce themselves to bony gesture
and the woods echo the hues of earth
itself, the colors of the light must feed
our eye's hunger, the ruddy sun of winter.

In early spring, we look down for color,
we look for the green of skunk cabbage,
golden crocuses along the south wall,
the small ears of violets unfolding.
Before the snows that glaze and magnify,
glitter and transmute, we look upward.
Great Chinese peonies float over the bay
splendid, bronzed by the light rebounding
from the water. In November we gaze up
into the stormy garden of the clouds.
What comes to us rides on the wind
and we face into it like gulls, waiting.

I have always been poor at flirting

I know it's harmless. My friends who flirt
the hardest—consummate, compulsive—are least
apt to fall into bed on a hot night's wind.
Flirting is what they do instead of sex,
five-year affairs of eyes and telephone trysts,
voices soft as warm taffy, artful laughs,
a hush when the spouse walks through the room.

Yet when I flirt I feel like an elephant
in a pink tutu balancing on a beach ball,
a tabby wearing a doll's dress, stuffed
in a carriage, about to snarl and slash.
I am pretending to be a girl, a girly girl.
A smile hangs on my face like a loose shutter.
My voice is petroleum jelly on my tongue.

My mother flirted with the milkman, the iceman,
the butcher—oh he winked and strutted,
flashing his gold tooth and slapping the scale.
Ogling, the plumber fixed both leaks
for the price of one. She flirted with the mailman,
the paperboy who brought our paper and only ours
to the door. I'd watch sour as a rotten lemon,

dour as a grandfather clock, cringing, muttering
Mother! like the curse word it was. The walls
would drip perfumed oil. The ceiling sagged buttery.
Her eyes were screwed wide open, Betty Boop,
batting butterfly wings, her mouth pursed,
while she played them like saxophones,
her voice now a tiny plush mouse,

now sleeking into the lower registers
of dark honey lapping at the belly.
When we couldn't pay the mortgage, she almost
climbed into the bank manager's lap.
Motorcycle cops pulling over our sputtering car,
teachers, principals, my father's bosses,
she had only one weapon, shameless silent

promises redeemable for absolutely nothing
but an ego job on the spot, frothing over.
If afterward she called them *behayma,*
fool, it was with quiet satisfaction,
an athlete who has performed well and won.
I remember the puzzled damaged look in her
widened eyes when flirting began to fail.

For some it is a drug of choice,
a moment's cocaine spiking the ego, giving
that spurt of a mirror cooing attraction.
For me it means only, I am powerless,
you can hurt or help me, wedged there above,
so I attempt this awkward dance of the broken
fan and the mud colored bubble, among your teeth.

Attraction to me is a walking toward,
the doors in the hands and the mind slowly
swinging on their hinges so that something
can pass over and something new enter.
This flicking of the body like a cape before
a bull, this mincing of the hook under
the feathers is more war and less love than I need.

It ain't heavy, it's my purse

We have marsupial instincts, women
who lug purses as big as garbage igloos,
women who hang leather hippos from their shoulders:

we are hiding the helpless greedy naked worms
of our intentions shivering in chaos.
In bags the size of Manhattan studio apartments,

we carry not merely the apparatus of neatness
and legality, cards, licenses, combs,
mirrors, spare glasses, lens fluid,

but hex signs against disaster and loss.
Antihistamines—if we should sneeze.
Painkillers—suppose the back goes out.

On my keyring, flats I used to stay in,
a Volvo I traded in 1985, two unknown doors
opening on what I might sometime direly need.

Ten pens, because the ink may run out.
Band-Aids, safety pins, rubber bands, glue,
maps, a notebook in case, addresses of friends

estranged. So we go hopping lopsided, women
like kangaroos with huge purses bearing
our own helplessness and its fancied cures.

Your father's fourth heart attack

The phone cord is the umbilicus
that binds him dying, shriveled,
to you his first son.
You try to draw him to you.
You give him advice. I hear

your voice tender, careful,
admonishing, arguing.
You ask him ten polite ways
why he is killing himself
by the teaspoonful, by the drop,

by the puff. Why he eats
ashes instead of apples,
why he sucks on death's
icy dry tit, why he turns
his face into darkness.

You cajole him, a step, a step
like a father coaxing a toddler,
but he falls through your fingers
into a maze of knives giving him
his face back screaming.

Twelve hours a day he worked,
four hours commuting, up nights
in a chair by TV late show light
wolfing burnt steak and salami on rye,
counting other men's paychecks.

He lived among men with boats,
sleek men, slick men, always richer.
He bought a boat from a moneyed neighbor,
fiberglass hulled, had it repaired,
started it, roared out and sank.

No place he lived was ever right,
but he was always talking up the next
move. He quarreled with brothers,
mother, friends, son, in-laws,
everyone except the bosses he twisted

and wrung himself to please.
He was always hungry. If he ate five
sandwiches, his hunger still knocked
on his bones like a broken radiator
and he was never full.

He lived a hunger bigger than a man,
a hunger to be other, golden,
a hollowness finally now filled
with pain. He holds you in the phone
but his eyes seek the dark in the mirror.

He slips in and out of his death bed
like a suit he keeps trying on, refitting.
He grabs at a hand and speaks the wrong
name, and the hand flops cold as a fish
while he calls till hoarseness, for himself.

Up and out

I. THE FOOT GNAWED OFF

We occupy neighborhoods like roominghouses.
The Irish lived here; the Italians, then the Jews,
then the Blacks up from the South and now
the Vietnamese fill this dirty decaying motel.
Nobody imagines staying. Success means getting out.

To be in a place then is only a move in a game;
who can love a box on a board? Remaining
is being stuck. My parents amused themselves
all through my childhood by choosing houses
from the Sunday paper to visit.

They could not afford to buy but pretended.
They wanted to walk through the large rooms
of their fantasies criticizing the wallpaper,
counting other people's chairs, imagining
waking in that bedroom on that street.

How can we belong to ourselves, when home
is something to pry yourself out of
like a pickup stuck on a sand road;
when what holds you has to be sacrificed
as a fox will gnaw off a foot to be free.

Growing up, what you love most can trap you.
Friends are for discarding. Lovers
for saying goodbye. Marriage looks like a closet.
Even your faithful dog could slow you down.
Polish your loneliness until its headlight shines.

Always what formed you, those faces
that hung like ripe apples in the tree
of your childhood: the hands that caressed you,
whose furtive touch untied the knot of pleasure
and loosened your flesh till it fluttered

and streamed with joy; those who taught you
fear at the end of a bright knife; who taught
you patience as their lips fumbled to force into
sounds strange squiggles blurring on the page;
who taught you guile as the hand teases the eye

into illusion; who gave you the names you really
use for the parts of your body, for the rush
of your anger hard into your teeth and fists;
always what formed you will come trailing guilt
like a cloud of fine ashes from burnt hair.

You will always be struck into memory like a match
spurting and then burn out in silence, because
there is no one to say, yes, I too remember,
I know how it was. We litter our past
on the sides of roads in fast food wrappers.

2. SOFT COAL COUNTRY
We used to drive to Ebensburg in the soft coal
country of Pennsylvania, an old brick Victorian
on the bottom of High Street where trucks shifted gears
to start their descent or labored upward all night;
from the backbone of High the ribs of side streets
like a fish carcass fell sharply away into gullies.
Around it were the miners' towns it served,
the grim company towns with the made-up names, Revloc,
Colver; the miners' shanties clinging to the sides
of hogback ridges, Nantiglo, Monday's Corner.

All the roads were blasted through rock.
On Horseshoe Curve you could watch the long long
freights toiling up and shrieking down, miles
around the crescent. The mountains had an anger
in them. The stone oozed bright water stained
with iron. I muttered the names of towns like prayers
returning with my father because a man must visit
his family. This was a place he had to leave,
so afraid of ending up with all grandmother's Lloyds
grubbing in the mines that when they shone

their sweet smiles at weddings, funerals, he'd
pretend he could not tell cousin from cousin.

Later when the mines shut and all the first
and second cousins were out of work for the fifth
year running and their families cracking along
old troubles, where they'd been glued, he said,
See, you can't make an honest living here.

I loved the mountains; he merely conquered them.
He returned not to see but to be seen, wearing
his one good suit, driving his nearly new car,
showing off the sexy black-haired wife not like any
in his high school yearbook, although they all knew
to sniff and say, Jew. Always the morning we left
he was up an hour early, tapping his foot under
the table, lighting cigarette from half-smoked butt
and then he would stomp his foot on the accelerator
and take the mountain roads clocking himself against
some pursuing maw so that if he did not push the car
and himself to the edge of danger, he would be back,
back with his desperate nagging sisters counting pennies
with a mountain on his chest pinning him down.

3 · WHEN I WAS CADDY

Cleveland was the promised land of my childhood,
where my bubba cooked kosher and even her cat had good
manners and sat at the table, and she told me that
when they were alone, he used a knife and fork.
I always hoped he would do it while I was eating.

I remember the smell of the women when I pressed
against her side behind the mehitzeh, camphor,
eucalyptus, cinnamon, lavender, sweat. Aunt Ruth
was the smartest girl, closer in age to me
than to my mother. When I was ten she married

into the middle class and took Bobbah to the suburbs.
She worked for the Navy. What a pity you don't
have a degree, they were always telling her,
but she did the work without a rating. Driven
to excel, she began to replace all the bowling

trophies with golfing trophies. We walked to
the course through the flat green morning swishing
with sprinklers, both of us almost tiptoeing. It was
so clean and neat, the streets like a funeral parlor
full of gladiolus, we tried to talk softly, properly.

All grandma's cronies were back in the ghetto.
There was no synagogue for miles. No kosher butcher.
She ate a lot of canned salmon and packaged soup.
Without neighbors to gossip about important things
she turned to the soaps and worried about Helen Trent.

Suddenly my mother was taking phone calls at 1 a.m.
she was warning, Do you want to lose it all?
So he hit you. So what else is new to wives?
Then Bobbah and Ruth were back in the ghetto,
now partly Black and Bobbah was cooking again.

The kitchen smelled the way it should and so did she.
Old ladies were drinking tea in glasses and quoting
Lenin and their own rabbis. Every strike was fought over.
Every young woman's reputation was put through a sieve.
Every grandchild was taken and properly raised.

And me, I was back, oh briefly, briefly back
in the promised land of love and endless stories
before cancer ate Bobbah, savoring each organ
but leaving her voice till the end. And Aunt Ruth
ran till she came to the Pacific and then fell down.

4. TOWARD A GOOD ROOTING MEDIUM

The Ogibwa said to me, my people have lived
on this sea since the mountains moved.
(The last ice age.) Our heart is here.
When we move to the cities, we blow into dust.

There are villages in Cornwall
continuously occupied for five thousand years.
Jericho has been a city since. 7000 B.C.E.
I've known families who farmed their soil

and gave their bones to it till it was as known
to them as the face of a mother or the body
of one passionately loved; people who have come back
to the same place year after year and retired on it,

walking its seasons till they can read the sky
like a personal letter; fisherman who could taste
a stream and tell you what the trout were doing.
This is not a pastoral: once I loved Manhattan so.

A friend could walk Paris streets on a map, sketching
the precise light, the houses, the traffic sounds.
Perhaps we should practice by loving a lilac bush.
Practice on a brick, an oriole nest, a tire of petunias.

O home over the expressway under a sky like something
you step in and scrape off your boot, heaped
ashtray we are stubbed into with smoldering butts,
billboards touting cancer under the carbolic rain!

Will the Lenni Lenape take back New Jersey?
The fish glow in the dark thrashing in dying
piles on every chenille bedspread, a light by which
we can almost read the fine print on the ceiling.

Love it because you can't leave it. Love it
or kill it. What we throw away returns in the blood
and leaves a chemical stain on the cell walls.
Huck honey, there's no territory to light out to.

That glow is from refineries on the farther shore.
Take your trash out with you or hunker down.
This is the Last Chance Saloon and Health Spa.
In heaven as on earth the dishes must be done.

The task never completed

No task is ever completed,
only abandoned or pressed into use.
Tinkering can be a form of prayer.

Twenty-six botched worlds preceded
Genesis we are told in ancient commentary,
and ha Shem said not only,

of this particular attempt
It is good, but muttered,
if only it will hold.

Incomplete, becoming, the world
was given us to fix, to complete
and we've almost worn it out.

My house was hastily built,
on the cheap. Leaks, rotting
sills, the floor a relief map of Idaho.

Whenever I get some money, I stove
up, repair, add on, replace.
This improvisation permits me to squat

here on the land that owns me.
We evolve through mistakes, wrong
genes, imitation gone wild.

Each night sleep unravels me into wool,
then into sheep and wolf. Walls and fire
pass through me. I birth stones.

Every dawn I stumble from the roaring
vat of dreams and make myself up
remembering and forgetting by halves.

Every dawn I choose to take a knife
to the world's flank or a sewing kit,
rough improvisation, but a start.

What are big girls made of?

The construction of a woman:
a woman is not made of flesh
of bone and sinew
belly and breasts, elbows and liver and toe.
She is manufactured like a sports sedan.
She is retooled, refitted and redesigned
every decade.

Cecile had been seduction itself in college.
She wriggled through bars like a satin eel,
her hips promising, her mouth pursed
in the dark red lipstick of desire.

She visited in '68 still wearing skirts
tight to the knees, dark red lipstick,
while I danced through Manhattan in mini skirt
lipstick pale as apricot milk,
hair loose as a horse's mane. Oh dear,
I thought in my superiority of the moment,
whatever has happened to poor Cecile.
She was out of fashion out of the game,
disqualified, disdained, dis-
membered from the club of desire.

Look at pictures in French fashion
magazines of the 18th century:
century of the ultimate lady
fantasy wrought of silk and corseting.
Paniers bring her hips out three feet
each way, while the waist is pinched
and the belly flattened under wood.
The breasts are stuffed up and out
offered like apples in a bowl.
The tiny foot is encased in a slipper

never meant for walking.
On top is a grandiose headache:
hair like a museum piece, daily
ornamented with ribbons, vases,
grottoes, mountains, frigates in full
sail, balloons, baboons, the fancy
of a hairdresser turned loose.
The hats were rococo wedding cakes
that would dim the Las Vegas strip.
Here is a woman forced into shape
rigid exoskeleton torturing flesh:
a woman made of pain.

How superior we are now:
see the modern woman
thin as a blade of scissors.
She runs on a treadmill every morning,
fits herself into machines of weights
and pulleys to heave and grunt,
an image in her mind she can never
approximate, a body of rosy
glass that never wrinkles,
never grows, never fades. She
sits at the table closing her eyes to food
hunger, always hungry
a woman made of pain.

A cat or dog approaches another,
they sniff noses. They sniff behinds.
They bristle or lick. They fall
in love as often as we do,
as passionately. But they fall
in love or lust with furry flesh,
not silicon breasts or push up bras
rib removal or liposuction.
It is not for male or female dogs
that poodles are clipped
to topiary hedges.

If only we could like each other raw.
If only we could love ourselves
like healthy babies burbling in our arms.

If only we were not programmed and reprogrammed
to need what is sold us.
Why should we want to live inside ads?
Why should we want to scourge our softness,
to straight lines like a Mondrian painting?
Why should we punish each other with scorn
as if to have a large ass
were worse than being greedy or mean?

When will women not be compelled
to view their bodies as science projects,
gardens to be weeded,
dogs to be trained?
When will a woman cease
to be made of pain?

Elegy in rock, for Audre Lorde

A child, I cherished a polyhedron of salt
my father brought up from under Detroit,
the pure crystal from a deep mine.
The miracle was it felt hard and clear
as glass and yet the tongue said tears.

My other treasure was a polished shard
of anthracite that glittered on my palm,
harder, fiercer than the soft coal
we shoveled into the basement furnace.
Coal halfway to a diamond?

More than once we talked about rocks
for which you had a passion, curiosity
fired by adventure, reading the landscape
with eye and pick, cliffs that confided
in a lover's whisper their history.

Obsidian, the obvious: it can take
an edge, can serve as a knife
in ritual or in combat, as your fine
dark deep voice could pour out love
or take an edge like a machete.

Carnelian lips, black and rose marble
metamorphosed rock blasted into beauty:
but what you are now that only the work
remains is garnet, not a flashy
jewel, native, smoldering, female.

Garnet: the blackest red,
color of the inner woman, of deep sex,
color of the inside of the lid closed tight
while the eye still searches
for light in itself.

Sand is the residue,
the pulverized bones of mountains.
Here on the great beach in summer
the sea rolls over and bares
slabs of tawny sand that glitter:

little buffed worlds of garnet
pool like the shadows of old blood
under the sun's yellow stare.
On my palm they wink, this shading
like rouge stippling the sand.

You told me of a garnet big as a child's
head, you told me of garnets glowing
like women's stories pulled from the dust,
garnets you freed into the sun,
lying on your palm like summer nights.

Rich darkness I praise, dark richness,
the true color of a live pulsing heart,
blackberries in strong sunlight,
crow's colors, black tulip chalices,
the city sky glowering from the plain.

Audre, Audre, your work shines on the night
of the world, the blaze of your words
but your own female power and beauty
are gone, a garnet ground into powder
and dissolved in wine the earth drinks.

All systems are up

You dial and a voice answers.
After you have stammered a reply
into dead air, you realize
it cannot hear or know you.
The preprogrammed voice of a thing
addresses you as a retarded dog:

Press 0 if you wish to be connected
to emergency services. Press 1
to order a product. Press 2
to speak to an agent. Press 3
if you need assistance.
Have a nice day.

I press 3. I need information.
Another robot says, Press 1
if you wish to order a product.
Press 2 to speak to an agent
—who bleeds? Press 3 if
you need further assistance.

I press 3. The voice says,
You have pressed 3.
That is not a valid number.
Please press 4 and make
another choice. I press 4.
The canned voice speaks:

Press 3 if you desire euthanasia.
Press 2 if you wish to detonate.
Press 1 never to have been born.
Press 0 for universal Armageddon.
Have a nice day.

For two women shot to death in Brookline, Massachusetts

How dare a woman choose?
Choose to be pregnant
choose to be childless
choose to be lesbian
choose to have two lovers or none
choose to abort
choose to live alone
choose to walk alone
at night
choose to come and to go
without permission
without leave
without a man.

Consider a woman's blood
spilled on a desk,
pooled on an office floor,
an ordinary morning at work,
an ordinary morning of helping
other women choose
to be or not to be
pregnant.

A woman young and smiling
sitting at a desk
trying to put other woman at ease
now bleeds from five
large wounds, bleeding
from her organs
bleeding out her life.

A young man is angry at women
women who say no

women who say maybe and mean no
women who won't
women who do and they shouldn't.
If they are pregnant they are bad
because that proves
they did it with someone,
they did it
and should die.

A man gets angry with a woman who decides to leave him
who decides to walk off
who decides to walk
who decides.

Woman are not real to such men.
They should behave as meat.
Such men drag them into the woods
and stab them
climb in their windows and rape them
such men shoot them in kitchens
such men strangle them in bed
such men lie in wait
and ambush them in parking lots
such men walk into a clinic
and kill the first woman they see.

In harm's way:
meaning in the way of a man
who is tasting his anger
like rare steak.
A daily ordinary courage
doing what has to be done
every morning, every afternoon
doing it over and over
because it is needed
put them in harm's way.

Two women dying
because they did their job
helping other women survive.
Two women dead
from the stupidity of an ex–altar boy
who saw himself
as a fetus
who pumped his sullen fury
automatically
into the woman in front of him
twice, and intended more.

Stand up now and say No More.
Stand up now and say We will not
be ruled by crazies and killers,
by shotguns and bombs and acid.
We will not dwell in the caves of fear.
We will make each other strong.
We will make each other safe.
There is no other monument.

A day in the life

She is wakened at 4 a.m.
Of course she does not
pick up, but listens
through the answering machine
to the male voice promising
she will burn in hell.

At seven she opens her door.
A dead cat is hammered
to her porch: brown tabby.
Hit by a car, no collar.
She hugs her own Duke of Orange.
She cannot let him out.

She has her car locked
in a neighbor's garage,
safe from pipe bombs,
but she must walk there.
She drives to work
a circuitous guesswork route.

Outside the clinic three
men walk in circles with photos
of six-month fetuses.
They surround her car.
They are forbidden the parking
lot but police don't care.

They bang on her hood.
As she gets out, they bump
and jostle her. One thrusts
his sign into her face.
She protects her eyes.
Something hard strikes her back.

Inside she sighs. Turns on
the lights, the air
conditioning, the coffee
machine. The security system
is always on. The funds
for teenage contraception,

gone into metal detectors.
She answers the phone.
"Is this where you kill babies?"
The second call a woman
is weeping. The day begins.
A girl raped by her stepfather,

a harried mother with too
many children and diabetes,
a terrified teenager who does
not remember how it happened,
a woman with an injunction
against an abuser. All day

she takes their calls,
all day she checks them in,
takes medical histories,
holds hands, dries tears,
hears secrets and lies and
horrors, soothes, continues.

Every time a new patient
walks in, a tinny voice
whispers, is this the one
carrying a handgun, with
an automatic weapon, with
a knife? She sits exposed.

She answers the phone,
"I'm going to cut your throat,
you murderer." "Have
a nice day." A bomb threat

is called in. She has
to empty the clinic.

The police finally come.
There is no bomb. The
doctor tells her how they
are stalking his daughter.
Then she goes home to Duke.
Eats a late supper by the TV.

Her mother calls. Her
boyfriend comes over. She
cries in his arms. He is,
she can tell, getting tired
of her tears. Next morning
she rises and day falls

on her like a truckload
of wet cement. This is
a true story, this is
what I know of virtue,
this is what I know
of goodness in our time.

The grey flannel sexual harassment suit

The woman in the sexual harassment
suit should be a virgin
who attended church every Sunday,
only ten thousand miles on her
back and forth to the pew.
Her immaculate house is
bleached with chlorine tears.

The woman in the sexual harassment
suit should never have known
a man other than her father
who kissed her only
on the cheek, and the minister
who patted her head
with his gloves on.

The woman in the sexual harassment
suit is visited by female
angels only, has a platinum
hymen protected by Brinks,
is white of course as unpainted
plaster, naturally blonde
and speaks only English.

The woman in the sexual harassment
suit wears white cotton blouses
buttoned to the throat, small
pearl clip-on earrings,
grey or blue suits and one
inch heels with nylons.
Her nails and lips are pink.

If you are other than we have
described above, please do
not bother to complain.
You are not a lady.
We cannot help you.
A woman like you simply
cannot be harassed.

On guard

I want you for my bodyguard,
to curl round each other like two socks
matched and balled in a drawer.

I want you to warm my backside,
two S's snaked curve to curve
in the down burrow of the bed.

I want you to tuck in my illness,
coddle me with tea and chicken
soup whose steam sweetens the house.

I want you to watch my back
as knives wink in the thin light
and whips crack out from shelter.

Guard my body against dust and disuse,
warm me from the inside out,
lie over me, under me, beside me

in bed as the night's creek
rushes over our shining bones
and we wake to the morning fresh

and wet, a birch leaf just uncurling.
Guard my body from disdain as age
widens me like a river delta.

Let us guard each other until death,
with teeth, brain and galloping heart,
each other's rose red warrior.

The thief

Dina sent me a postcard,
history at a glance,
Sonka of the golden hand,
the notorious thief
being put in chains.

She looks young still, dark hair,
unsmiling—why would she?
1915, surrounded by Russian men
two blacksmiths preparing
the chains and three soldiers
to guard her, weaponless.

A Jew from Odessa, she could
move faster than water
as quiet as a leaf growing
more lightly than a shaft
of sun tapping your arm.

Like all young women
she was full of desires
little hot pomegranate seeds
bursting in her womb,
wishes crying from the dull
mirror of poverty.

Sonka heard the voices calling
from inside the coins,
take me, Sonka, take me
turn me into something sweet
turn me into something warm and soft
a cashmere shawl, a silk mantilla
a coat of fur like a bed of loving.

Eat me, said the chicken.
drink me, the brandy sang.
Wear me, the blouse whispered.

Sonka of the golden hands
stands in the grim yard
of the prison, with her quick
hands bound in iron bracelets
calling with her solemn eyes

let me go, oh you who stare
at me and jail me in your
camera, now at last
free me to dance again
as I freed
those captured coins.

Belly good

A heap of wheat, says the Song of Songs
but I've never seen wheat in a pile.
Apples, potatoes, cabbages, carrots
make lumpy stacks, but you are sleek
as a seal hauled out in the winter sun.

I can see you as a great goose egg
or a single juicy and fully ripe peach.
You swell like a natural grassy hill.
You are symmetrical as a Hopewell mound,
with the eye of the naval wide open,

the eye of my apple, the pear's port
window. You're not supposed to exist
at all this decade. You're to be flat
as a kitchen table, so children with
roller skates can speed over you

like those sidewalks of my childhood
that each gave a different roar under
my wheels. You're required to show
muscle striations like the ocean
sand at ebb tide, but brick hard.

Clothing is not designed for women
of whose warm and flagrant bodies
you are a swelling part. Yet I confess
I meditate with my hands folded on you,
a maternal cushion radiating comfort.

Even when I have been at my thinnest,
you have never abandoned me but curled

round as a sleeping cat under my skirt.
When I spread out, so do you. You like
to eat, drink and bang on another belly.

In anxiety I clutch you with nervous fingers
as if you were a purse full of calm.
In my grandmother standing in the fierce sun
I see your cauldron that held eleven children
shaped under the tent of her summer dress.

I see you in my mother at thirty
in her flapper gear, skinny legs
and then you knocking on the tight dress.
We hand you down like a prize feather quilt,
our female shame and sunburst strength.

The flying Jew

I never met my uncle Dave.
The most real thing I know about him
is how he died, which he did
again and again in the middle of the night
my mother screaming, my father shouting,
"Shut up, Bert, you're having a bad dream."

My uncle Dave, the recurring nightmare.
He was the Jew who flew.
How did he manage it? Flying was for
gentlemen, and he was a kid from the slums
of Philadelphia, Pittsburgh, Cleveland—
zaydeh one headlong leap ahead of the law
and the Pinkertons, the goons who finally
bashed his head in when he was organizing
his last union, the bakery workers.

Dave looked up between the buildings,
higher than the filthy sparrows who pecked
at horse dung and the pigeons who strutted
and cooed in the tenement eaves,
up to the grey clouds of Philadelphia,
the rust clouds of Pittsburgh with the fires
of the open hearth steel mills staining them,
a pillar of smoke by day and fire by night.

He followed into the clouds.
My mother doesn't know who taught
him to fly, but he learned.
He became one with the plane, they said.
Off he went to France. He flew in combat,
was shot down and survived, never

became an ace, didn't enjoy combat,
the killing, but flying was better than sex.

He took my mother up once and she wept
the whole time. She wouldn't fly again
till she was seventy-five and said then
she didn't care if the plane went down.

It was his only talent, his only passion
and a good plane was a perfect fit for
his body and his mind, his reflexes.
The earth was something that clung to his shoes,
something to shake off, something to gather
all your strength into a taut charge
and then launch forward and leave behind.

After the war, he was lost for two years,
tried selling, tried insurance, then off
he went barnstorming with his war buddies.
Time on the ground was just stalling time,
killing time, parked in roominghouses
and tourist homes and bedbug hotels.
He drank little. Women were aspirin.

Being the only Jew, he had something
to prove every day, so he flew the fastest,
he did the final trick that made the audience
shriek. The planes grew older, the crowds
thinned out. One fall day outside Cleveland
he got his mother, sister Bert and her
little boy to watch the act. It was a triple
Zimmerman roll he had done five hundred
shows but this time the plane plowed
into the earth and a fireball rose.

So every six months he died flaming
in the middle of the night, and all I
ever knew of him was Mother screaming.

My rich uncle, whom I only met three times

We were never invited to his house.
We went there once while they were all in Hawaii,
climbed steps from which someone had shoveled
the snow, not him, to the wide terrace.
Yellow brick, the house peered into fir and juniper.
It was too large for me to imagine what it held
but I was sure everyone of them, four girls
and bony wife, each had a room of her own.

He had been a magician and on those rare
nights he had to stay at the Detroit Statler
downtown, he would summon us for supper
in the hotel restaurant. Mother would put on
and take off every dress in her closet, all six,
climb in the swaybacked brown Hudson muttering shame.
He would do tricks with his napkin and pull
quarters from my ears and spoons from his sleeves.

He had been a clumsy acrobat, he had failed at comedy
and vaudeville; he was entertaining for a party
when he met a widow with four girls and an inheritance.
He waltzed right out of her romantic movie dreams
and he strolled into her house and she had him redone.
He learned to talk almost like her dead husband.
He learned to wear suits, play golf and give orders
to servants. His name changed, his background rebuilt,
his religion painted over, he almost fit in.

Of my uncles, only he was unreal, arriving by plane
to stay on the fanciest street in downtown Detroit.
The waiter brought a phone to the table, his broker
calling. I imagined a cowboy breaking horses.
He made knives disappear. He made a napkin vanish.
He was like an animated suit, no flesh, no emotions
bubbling the blood and steaming the windows as

my other uncles and aunts did. Only the discreet
Persian leather smell of money droned in my nose.

His longest trick was to render himself invisible.
Then one night after the guests had left, he went down
to the basement in the latest multilevel glass vast
whatnot shelf of house and hanged himself by the furnace.
They did not want his family at the funeral. She had
no idea, his wife said, why would he be depressed?
I remember his laugh like a cough and his varnished
face, buffed till the silverware shone in his eyes.
His last trick was to vanish himself forever.

Your standard midlife crisis

A friend is destroying his life
like a set of dishes
he has tired of, is breaking
for the noise.

The old wife is older
of course. She promises
nothing but what he knows
he can have.

She is an oak rocking chair,
sturdy, plain, shapely
something he has taken comfort
in for years.

This one flirts like a firefly,
on and off, on and off.
Where will she flash next?
In his pocket.

She mirrors his needs,
she sends him messages to decode
twisted in his hair, knotted
in his skin.

With me you will forget failure.
With me you will be another.
My youth will shave your years
to smooth fresh skin.

O real life, I feel! he says,
his infatuation, a charge

like fourteen cups of espresso
and as lasting.

He careens downhill, throwing off
books, children, history,
tossing friends, pledges, knowledge
down into crystal canyon.

There every cliff reflects her
face with the eyes illuminating
him like fireworks, doomed
to burn themselves out.

The visitation

The yearling doe stands by the pile of salt
hay, nibbling and then strolls up the path.
Among the spring flowers she stands amazed,
hundreds of daffodils, forsythia,
the bright chalices of tulips, crimson,
golden, orange streaked with green, the wild
tulips opening like stars fallen on the ground.
She leans gracefully to taste a tarda,
yellow and white sunburst, sees us, stops,
uncertain. Stares at us with her head cocked.
What are you? She is not frightened
but bemused. Do I know you?
The landscaping dazzles her, impresses her
far more than the two of us on the driveway
speaking to her in the same tone we use
with the cats as if she had become our pet,
as she sidles among the peach trees,
a pink blossom clinging to her dun flank.

Graceful among the rhododendrons, I know
what her skittish courage represents: she
is beautiful as those sub-Saharan children
with the huge luminous brown eyes of star-
vation. A hard winter following a hurricane,
tangles of downed trees even the deer
cannot penetrate, a long slow spring
with the buds obdurate as pebbles,
too much building, so she comes to stand
in our garden, eyes flowering with wonder
under the incandescent buffet of the fruit
trees, this garden cafeteria she has walked
into to graze, from the lean late woods.

Half vulture, half eagle

I saw it last night, the mortgage
bird with heavy hunched shoulders
nesting in shredded hundred dollar bills
its long curved claws seize, devour.

You feed it and feed it in hopes
it will grow smaller. Does this make
sense? After five years of my writing
checks on the first day of every month

it is swollen and red eyed and hungry.
It has passed from owner to owner,
sold by the bank to Ohio and thence
to an ersatz company that buys up slave

mortgages and is accountable to Panama
or perhaps Luxembourg, cannot be
communicated with by less than four lawyers
connected end to end like Christmas

tree light sets and blinking in six
colors simultaneously by fax.
It says, I squat on the foot of your
bed when the medical bills shovel in.

When your income withers like corn
stalks in a Kansas drought, I laugh
with a sound of sand hitting a windshield,
laughter dry as parched kernels from which

all water has been stolen by the sun.
Each month I wring you a little more.
I own a corner of your house, say
the northeast corner the storms hit

when they roar from the blast of the sea
churned into grey sudsy cliffs, and as
the storm bashes the dunes into sand
it washes away, so I can carry off

your house any time you fail to feed
me promptly. Your misfortune is my
best gamble. I am the mortgage bird
and my weight is on your back.

The level

A great balance hangs in the sky
and briefly on the black pan
and on the blue pan, the melon
of the moon and the blood orange
of the sun are symmetrical
like two unmatched eyes glowing
at us with one desire.

This is an instant's equality,
a level that at once
starts to dip. In spring
the sun starts up its golden
engine earlier each dawn.
In fall, night soaks
its dye into the edges of day.

But now they hang, two bright
balls teasing us to balance
the halves of our brain, need
and will, gut and intellect,
you and me in an instant's grace—
understanding no woman, even
Gaia, can always make it work.

The negative ion dance

The ocean reopens us.
The brass doors in the forehead swing wide.
Light enters us like a swarm of bees
and bees turn into white petals falling.

The lungs expand as the salt air
stretches them, and they sing, treble
bagpipes eerie and serpentine.
The bones lighten to balsa wood.

The head bobs on air currents
like a bright blue balloon without ballast.
The arms want to flap. The terns
dive around us giving hopeless instruction.

Light is sharp, serrated, a flight of saws.
Light enters us and is absorbed like water,
like radiation. We take the light in
and darken it. We look just the same.

We shine only in the back of the eyes
if you stare into them as you kiss.
The light leaks out through the palms
as they caress you later in the dark.

The voice of the grackle

Among the red winged blackbirds—
latecomers clustered at the top
of the sugar maple after the others
have split up the better home sites
in the marshes, along Dun's Run—
their buzzes, chirs and warbles,
I hear a rasp, a harsh ruckus.

The grackles have come north again.
Nobody greets them with the joy
meted out to robins, the geese
rowing high overhead, the finches
flitting gold and red to the feeders.
I am their solitary welcoming
committee, tossing extra corn.

Their cries are no more melodious
than the screech of unadjusted
brakes, and yet I like their song
of the unoiled door hinge creaking,
the rusty saw grating, the squawk
of an air mattress stomped on,
unmistakable among the twitters.

They are big and shiny, handsome
even sulking in the rain.
Feathers gleam like the polish
on a new car when the sun hits them,
black as asphalt, with oil slick
colors shimmering, purple satin
like hoods in their gang colors.

We never see more than a few,
often one alone, like the oversized
kid who hangs out, misfit, with
the younger crowd, slumps at the back
of the classroom making offcolor
comments in his cracking voice,
awkward, half clown, half hero.

Salt in the afternoon

The room is a conch shell
and echoing in it, the blood
rushes in the ears,
the surf of desire sliding in
on the warm beach.

The room is the shell of the moon
snail, gorgeous predator
whose shell winds round and round
the color of moonshine
on your pumping back.

The bed is a slipper shell
on which we rock, opaline
and pearled with light sweat,
two great deep currents
colliding into white water.

The clamshell opens.
The oyster is eaten.
The squid shoots its white ink.
Now there is nothing but warm
salt puddles on the flats.

Brotherless one: Sun god

In a family snapshot I stand in pigtails
grinning. I hug the two pillars
of my cracked world, my cold
father, my hot brother, the fair and the ruddy,
the grey eyed forbidder, the one who hit
but never caressed, who shouted
but never praised; and on the left, you.
You were the dark pulsating sun of my childhood,
the man whose eyes could give water
instead of ice, eyes brown as tree bark.

You were the one I looked like, as even
your children looked more like me
than like their mothers. All had the same
dark slanted Tartar eyes glinting like blades
and the same black hair rippling—
coarse, abundant, grass of a tundra of night.
We are small and scrappy.
We go for the throat in anger.
We have bad genes and good minds.
We drag a load of peacock tales sweeping the dust.

Myths come into life around us
like butterflies hatching, bright and voracious.
We learned sex easily as we learned to talk
and it shaped our handshakes and our laughter.
Trouble was our shadow, tied to our heels.

Thus we grew out of the same mother
but never spoke real words since I turned twelve.
Yet you built into my psyche that space
for a man not of ice and thumbtacks,
a man who could think with his body,
a man who could laugh from the soles
of his feet, a man who could touch
skin simply as sun does.
You gave me a license
for the right of the body to joy.

Brotherless two: Palimpsest

My friend Elizabeth said, the week you died
and your widow would not have me at
your funeral, you and your brother:
both had great wild imaginations.
You put yours into books.
He rewrote himself.

I can remember the last honest talking that ever
went between us, strong, jolting to me
as straight bourbon to a child not used to beer.

You were just back from the war,
still a Marine, crazy on experimental
drugs for malaria, and you poured
the whole Pacific war into my ears
till I was raw and blistered.
Forty years later I could hear your voice,
I could see the women falling into the sea,
I could see the rotting bodies on the coral,
I remember your talking of the smell of battle,
of shit when bodies break open,
how blood stinks like spoiled meat.

You talked about how you had been promoted
then busted for hitting your sergeant,
time in stockade, beaten for being
a Jew, for being short, for having
a temper like a piñata breaking.

You were back to divorce Florence,
your second wife. You brought souvenirs
of the occupation, silks, a kimono,
glass animals, little saki cups, photos

of you with buddies, geishas, captured flags.
You marched on and on as the medicine burned
in you. I was the pit into which you shoveled
memories and then walked off.

You winked at me and you began to whistle.
In your mind you began to change the sky,
the water, the land. The stories turned
from yellow to blue. The blood turned
to paint. It smelled like glory.
It was the Fourth of July all year
and the war became a recruiting poster
featuring you.

Brotherless three: Never good enough

Suzie was my niece; she was not
your daughter: you refused her
the way someone will send back the wrong
dish in a restaurant.
The way you turned from the sons
of your third marriage. In a pique
you had a vasectomy, saying that no child
of yours ever did it right.

Did what? You seemed to have no love
to spare for them, as you pretended
your first three wives were one
dead woman. For twelve years
we had only an occasional card.

What is a half brother? Half time?
Half there? Half brother and half not?
We had different fathers. Yours, a short
stocky Jew whom imigration had labeled
a foot itch product, Courtade. The
year before your bar mitzvah, our mother
eloped with my father. Your father
took out her desertion on you.

When you were sixteen, my parents
caught you fucking your girlfriend Isabel,
forced you to marry. They tried
that on me at eighteen. I yelled
I'd take off and she'd never see me again.
A pit lined with fur and barbed wire;
roast chicken and plastique, warmth
and bile, a kiss and a razor in the ribs,
our family.

These memories tangle, a fine gold chain
with invisible barbs. As I pick out knots,

always there are tighter knots inside.
My fingers bleed. I remember
coming to see you in L.A. in '64.
I was in civil rights. Black friends
told me L.A. was bad, stewing, smell of raw
sewage on smoggy mornings, hope eviscerated.
You said, We have no Negroes here.

Each link, a barb. Each set of links,
a knot I could never pick free.
My palms are crisscrossed with scars
as from barbed wire.

By then you were a college graduate—
who had not finished high school.
By then, your father was a Frenchman,
a French Catholic. By then, you were
a Marine hero with medals and war stories
you shared at the VFW. You drank martinis
instead of boilermakers. You speculated
in real estate near that huge
stinking sink the Salton Sea
where drowned rats wash up by the flooded
motels and the desert is laid out
with sidewalks and street signs.

Once when I read poetry in your city
you came. Afterward you stared at me.
Why do you remember those old sad things?
Why do these people come to hear you?
That old stuff, who cares?
Ah, but you cared. You could not look
me in the eyes. You could not risk
one real word
for fear I would like a big bad wolf
blow your house down
with my voice of fire.

Brotherless four: Liars dance

The myth says, he left three women,
three children, his family; his best friend
he left to die alone, so he was lonely
and unloved to the bitter end.

We live far more in fractals than in grids.
His fourth wife was Chicana, a widow
with four children who had a house
in a good section of the L.A. hills.
Of all his wives and girlfriends,
she alone resembled our mother—
small, dark, busty, flirtatious
she smiled easily and lied,
as well as he did, but not to him.

She was Spanish, an old colonial
family; he was French.
They were passionate to be proper.
Their house was papered with genealogies,
an aristocracy of Oz, detailed
as the papers of a prize schnauzer,
a past elaborated, documented
with the zeal of federal marshals
protecting a star witness.

Maybe I should simply see it
as a mating dance, two cranes
stepping about each other transfixed,
the ritual of two hot lovers
in bed pretending to be children
or Klingons or dogs—extending
the role for thirty years.
Like lovebirds in a cage,
they did not tire of the mirror
or each other.

Brotherless five: Truth as a cloud of moths

In adolescence I tried on others'
styles, shrugged on a leather coat
of tough street kid I had thrown off
to run the college marathon;
turned existentialist in black
turtleneck and black jeans;
played vamp, played Romeo
and Juliet alternate nights.
I would copy bits from movies,
wriggle my hips like this one,
pout like that. I thrust myself
into dramas and slithered out.

I've always seen the alternate
lives, the faces I might have worn
had I left the party with this man
or that instead of going alone
into the night's soft rumble;
had I paused when the golden balls
were thrown before me on the race
course like Atalanta, instead
of laughing and running on.

Variant selves haunt
the corridors of my brain, people
my novels, crowd in like ghosts
drawn to blood when friends
or strangers tell me secrets
hand me their troubles,
sweaters knit of hair and wire.

Why then have I stalked for years
round and round the self you
built of forged documents,
charm, sweat and subterfuge
as if I were the sentinel of truth?
We both wrote ourselves into being.

Brotherless six: Unconversation

I buzz irritating and persistent
darting, biting at your death.
What do I hope to understand?
Why I grieve for someone I did not know?

I was a white cedar swamp you traversed
on a wooden walkway above the black water.
You were a closet from which odd toys
and bizarre tools fell out on my head.

Our conversations were conducted
without a common language.
I gave you a foot. You handed me a balloon.
You gave me spurs. I passed you marmalade.

You thought I bore the past
like a broad sword swinging
to cleave you from your fictions
and perhaps you were right.

I'm an impolite wind that blows umbrellas
wrong side to. Now I make you up
out of pain you deposited in me decades
ago, eggs of blood red dragonflies.

I put out stories like weird fruit,
a cheap mail order novelty: GROW PEACHES
PLUMS, KIWIS, APPLES ON THE SAME TREE.
Grandma's tales, mother's, friends' and strangers':

you are stirred and mixed with them
in the incandescent melting pot of my mind.
I mother you into new ferment
who would not brother me.

Brotherless seven: Endless end

I have trouble understanding
when something is done
that was not finished.

I have to let you go
since I lack a hold,
no connection beyond a history

you had abandoned
like worn out clothes
delivered to Goodwill.

Lives are full of broken dishes
and promises, stories left
half told, apologies

that come back like letters
with insufficient postage,
keys that open no known doors.

The abandoned live with an absence
that shaped them like the canyon
of a river gone dry.

Do I mourn you, Phoenix hedonist,
or the man in the mirror
you killed in 1945,

because he was dragging you down?
I have made my own brothers,
my sisters. It is hard

to say goodbye to nothing
personal, mouthfuls bitten off
of silence and wet ashes.

from
Early Grrrl

The correct method of worshipping cats

For her name is, She who must be petted.
For her name is, She who eats from the flowered plate.
For her name is, She who wants the door always opened.
For her name is, She who must sleep between your legs.

And he is called, He who must be played with until he drops.
He is called, He who can wail loudest of all.
He is called, He who eats also from your plate.
He is called, He who sleeps in the softest chair.

And they are known as eaters and rollers in catnip
Famous among the nations for resonant purring.
Feared among the mouse multitudes. The voles
and moles also do run from their shadow.

For they perform cossack dances at 4 a.m.
For they stick their faces in your face and meow.
For they sit on the computer monitor to monitor your work.
For they make you laugh with their silly acrobatics

but their dignity is that of the oldest gods.
Because of all this we are permitted to serve them.
We are the cat servants, some well trained and some ill,
and they give us nothing but love and trouble.

The well preserved man

He was dug up from a bog
where the acid tanned him
like a good leather workboot.

He is complete, teeth, elbows,
toenails and stomach, penis,
the last meal he was fed.

Sacrificed to a god or goddess
for fertility, good weather,
an end to a plague, who knows?

Only he was fed and then killed,
as I began to realize as you
ordered the expensive wine,

urged lobster or steak, you
whose eyes always toted the bill,
I was to be terminated that night.

I could not eat my last meal.
I kept running to the ladies room.
All I could do was drink and try,

try not to weep at the table.
I was green as May leaves opening wetly,
I was new as a never folded dollar,

a child who didn't know how the old
story always ended. Sacrificed
to a woman with more to offer,

the new May queen, lady of prominent
family, like the bog man I was
strangled with little bruising.

I lay in my bed with arms folded
believing my life had bled out.
How astonished I was to survive,

to find I was intact and hungry.
All that happened was I knew the story
now and I grew long nails and teeth.

Nightcrawler

Easy sleepers tucked in their white envelopes
with a seal that only dawn's alarm will break:
with envy I lift away the sides of houses.
Their snores arise like furry incense.

Shunted like a boxcar through broken switches
I rattle down prairie ghostlands of remember
past rusty flyblown sagging shingle towns
where the rusty sign of want creaks in the wind.

Floodlit by a blind eyeball of moon,
the past here is continuously performed,
an all night movie for insomniacs.
The floor is sticky with candy or with blood.

Voyeur, I spy on my own dead, in action.
Glued to that dim keyhole, I shout at them
Hold on! Put down that bottle. Toss those pills.
Next week a love letter will come with a check.

They don't listen. They break each other's
bones. They rub ground glass into their eyes
as blood flows out like satin under the door.
Always a phone rings in an empty house.

Easy sleepers, do ghosts ride your rails
all night telling stories you dread hearing?
This train runs backward toward old deaths
as fast as I pull forward toward new ones.

I vow to sleep through it

I hate New Year's Eve.
I remember the panic to have
something, anything to do,
some kind of date
animal, vegetable, mineral,
a giant walking carrot,
a boa constrictor, a ferret,
an orangutan, a lump of coal.

I remember ringing apartment
bells on 114th Street
looking for a rumored party.
Parties with lab punch:
Mogen David, grapefruit juice
and lab alcohol, hangovers
guaranteed to anyone within
ten yards of the foaming punchbowl.

I wake the next morning
with my mouth full of mouse
turds and wood ashes.
I wake and remember
how I tried to demonstrate
the hula, my hips banging
like a misloaded washer,
how I made out with a toad.

I remember limp parties,
parties askew, everyone
straggling home with the wrong
mate, the false match.
Evenings endless and boring
as a bowling tournament
at the senior center.
Is it midnight yet?

Only 9:30? Only
9:38? At midnight
we will spill drinks on
each other's clothes, kiss
the boors and bores we detest,
the new year like a white
tablecloth on which a drink
has already been spilled.

Midsummer night's stroll

The attenuated silvery evenings of northern summer,
they are at once languid and fierce, white Persian
cats preparing to mate. They are pale lilies
whose fragrance paints the air of a bedroom.

The light is milky, suave and must be entered.
Who can sit inside with the lights on?
This mauve sky wants to soak through your skin.
Your body will float like a cherry blossom fallen

on a slowly moving mirroring river.
This glow will not tan but lighten your flesh
till you find yourself borne up as pollen.
Words escape you like birds startled awake.

Your lover's face floats on this dusk, an alien
moon. You rise and vanish in the sky like a balloon.

The name of that country is lonesome

We go to meet our favorite programs
the way we might have met a lover,
the mixture of the familiar routine
and the unexpected revelation.

We can buy love at the shelter
if we get there before they have
executed it for being unwanted,
its fur cooling in the garbage.

It becomes more and more unusual
to be invited to dinner;
fast food is the family feast.
Who can be bothered with friends?

They have needs, you have to remember
their birthdays, they want to talk
when you're just too tired.
Leave the answering machine on.

No one comes to the door any longer.
We would be scared.
That's why we have an alarm.
That's why we keep the gun loaded.

Drive-in food, drive-in teller,
drive-by shooting, stay in the car.
Talk only to the television set.
It tells you just what to buy

so you won't feel lonely
any longer, so you won't feel
inadequate, bored, so you can
almost imagine yourself alive.

Always unsuitable

She wore little teeth of pearls around her neck.
They were grinning politely and evenly at me.
Unsuitable they smirked. It is true

I look a stuffed turkey in a suit. Breasts
too big for the silhouette. She knew
at once that we had sex, lots of it

as if I had strolled into her diningroom
in a dirty negligee smelling gamy
smelling fishy and sporting a strawberry

on my neck. I could never charm
the mothers, although the fathers ogled
me. I was exactly what mothers had warned

their sons against. I was quicksand.
I was trouble in the afternoon. I was
the alley cat you don't bring home.

Where I came from, the nights I had wandered
and survived, scared them, and where
I would go they never imagined.

Ah, what you wanted for your sons
were little ladies hatched from the eggs
of pearls like pink and silver lizards

cool, well behaved and impervious
to desire and weather alike. Mostly
that's who they married and left.

Oh, mamas, I would have been your friend.
I would have cooked for you and held you.
I might have rattled the windows

of your sorry marriages, but I would
have loved you better than you know
how to love yourselves, bitter sisters.

from
The Art of Blessing the Day

The art of blessing the day

This is the blessing for rain after drought:
Come down, wash the air so it shimmers,
a perfumed shawl of lavender chiffon.
Let the parched leaves suckle and swell.
Enter my skin, wash me for the little
chrysalis of sleep rocked in your plashing.
In the morning the world is peeled to shining.

This is the blessing for sun after long rain:
Now everything shakes itself free and rises.
The trees are bright as pushcart ices.
Every last lily opens its satin thighs.
The bees dance and roll in pollen
and the cardinal at the top of the pine
sings at full throttle, fountaining.

This is the blessing for a ripe peach:
This is luck made round. Frost can nip
the blossom, kill the bee. It can drop,
a hard green useless nut. Brown fungus,
the burrowing worm that coils in rot can
blemish it and wind crush it on the ground.
Yet this peach fills my mouth with juicy sun.

This is the blessing for the first garden tomato:
Those green boxes of tasteless acid the store
sells in January, those red things with the savor
of wet chalk, they mock your fragrant name.
How fat and sweet you are weighing down my palm,
warm as the flank of a cow in the sun.
You are the savor of summer in a thin red skin.

This is the blessing for a political victory:
Although I shall not forget that things
work in increments and epicycles and sometime
leaps that half the time fall back down,
let's not relinquish dancing while the music

fits into our hips and bounces our heels.
We must never forget, pleasure is real as pain.

The blessing for the return of a favorite cat,
the blessing for love returned, for friends'
return, for money received unexpected;
the blessing for the rising of the bread,
the sun, the oppressed. I am not sentimental
about old men mumbling the Hebrew by rote
with no more feeling than one says *gesundheit*.

But the discipline of blessings is to taste
each moment, the bitter, the sour, the sweet
and the salty, and be glad for what does not
hurt. The art is in compressing attention
to each little and big blossom of the tree
of life, to let the tongue sing each fruit,
its savor, its aroma and its use.

Attention is love, what we must give
children, mothers, fathers, pets,
our friends, the news, the woes of others.
What we want to change we curse and then
pick up a tool. Bless whatever you can
with eyes and hands and tongue. If you
can't bless it, get ready to make it new.

Learning to read

My mother would not teach me to read.
Experts in newspapers and pop books
said school must receive us virgin.
Secrets were locked in those

black scribbles on white, magic
to open the sky and the earth.
In a book I tried to guess from
pictures, a mountain had in its side

a door through which children ran in
after a guy playing a flute
dressed all in green, and I too
wanted to march into a mountain.

When I sat at Grandmother's seder,
the book went around and everybody
read. I did not make a distinction
between languages. Half the words

in English were strange to me.
I knew when I had learned to read
all would be clear, I would know
everything that adults knew, and more.

Every handle would turn for me.
At school I grabbed words like toys
I had been denied. Finally I
could read, me. I read every sign

from the car. On journeys I read
maps. I read cereal boxes
and cans spelling out the hard words.
All printing was sacred.

At the seder I sat down at the table,
self-important, adult on my cushion.
I was no longer the youngest child
but the smartest. When the haggadah

was to be passed across me,
I grabbed it, roaring confidence.
But the squiggles, the scratches
were back. Not a letter

waved to me. I was blinded again.
That night I learned about tongues.
Grandma explained she herself spoke
Yiddish, Russian, Polish, Lithuanian

and bad English, little Hebrew.
That's okay, I said. I will
learn all languages. But I was
fifty before I read Hebrew.

I no longer expect to master
every alphabet before death
snatches away everything I know.
But they are always beckoning to me

those languages still squiggles
and noises, like lovers I never
had time to enjoy, places
I have never (yet) arrived.

Snowflakes, my mother called them

Snowflakes, my mother called them.
My grandmother made papercuts
until she was too blind to see
the intricate birds, trees, Mogen
Davids, moons, flowers
that appeared like magic
when the folded paper
was opened.

My mother made simpler ones,
abstract. She never saved them.
Not hers, not mine.
It was a winter game.
Usually we had only newsprint
to play with. Sometimes
we used old wrapping paper,
white sheets from the bakery.

Often Grandma tacked hers
to the walls or on the window
that looked on the street,
the east window where the sun
rose hidden behind tenements
where she faced to pray.
I remember one with deer,
delicate hooves, fine antlers

for Pesach. Her animals were
always in pairs, the rabbits,
the cats, always cats in pairs,
little mice, but never horses,
for horses meant pogrom,

the twice widowed woman's
sense of how things should be,
even trees by twos for company.

I had forgotten. I had lost it all
until a woman sent me a papercut
to thank me for a poem, and then
in my hand I felt a piece of past
materialize, a snowflake long melted,
evaporated, cohering and once
again long necked fragile deer
stood, made of skill and absence.

On Shabbat she dances in the candle flame

How we danced then, you can't imagine
my grandmother said. We danced
till we were dizzy, we danced
till the room spun like a dreydl,
we danced ourselves drunk and giddy,
we danced till we fell panting.

We were poor, my grandmother said,
a few potatoes, some half rotten
beans, greens from the hedgerow.
But then on Shabbat we ate a chicken.
The candles shone on the golden skin.
We drank sweet wine and flew up to the ceiling.

How I loved him, you can't imagine
my grandmother said. He was from St.
Petersburg, my father could scarcely
believe he was a Jew, he dressed so fine.
His eyes burned when he looked at me.
He quoted Pushkin instead of Mishnah.

Nine languages and still the Czar
wanted him in the Army, where Jews
went off but never returned.
My father married us from his deathbed.
We escaped the Pale under a load of straw.
You can't imagine, we were frightened mice.

Eleven children I bore, my grandmother said,
nine who grew up, four who died

before me. Now I sing in your ear.
When you pray I stand beside you.
Eliyahu's cup at the seder table is for
me, who cooked and never sat down:

now I sit enthroned on your computer.
Now I am the queen of dustmop tales,
I preside over your memory lighting
candles that summon the dead.
I touch your lids while you sleep
and when you wake, you imagine me.

In the grip of the solstice

Feels like a train roaring into night,
the journey into fierce cold just beginning.
The ground is newly frozen, the crust
brittle and fancy with striations,
steeples and nipples we break
under our feet.

Every day we are shortchanged a bit more,
night pressing down on the afternoon
throttling it. Wan sunrise later
and later, every day trimmed
like an old candle you beg to give
an hour's more light.

Feels like hurtling into vast darkness,
the sky itself whistling of space
the black matter between stars
the red shift as the light dies,
warmth a temporary aberration,
entropy as a season.

Our ancestors understood the brute
fear that grips us as the cold
settles around us, closing in.
Light the logs in the fireplace tonight,
light the candles, first one, then two,
the full hanikiya.

Light the fire in the belly.
Eat hot soup, cabbage and beef
borsch, chicken soup, lamb

and barley, stoke the marrow.
Put down the white wine and pour
whiskey instead.

We reach for each other in our bed
the night vaulted above us
like a cave. Night in the afternoon,
cold frosting the glass so it hurts
to touch it, only flesh still
welcoming to flesh.

Woman in a shoe

There was an old woman who lived
in a shoe, her own two shoes,
men's they were, brown and worn.
They flapped when she hobbled along.

There was an old woman who lived
in a refrigerator box under
the expressway with her cat.
January, they died curled together.

There was an old woman who lived
in a room under the roof. It
got hot, but she was scared
to open the window. It got hotter.

Too hot, too cold, too poor,
too old. Invisible unless
she annoys you, invisible
unless she gets in your way.

In fairy tales if you are kind
to an old woman, she gives you
the thing you desperately need:
an unconquerable sword, a purse

bottomless and always filled,
a magical ring. We don't believe
that anymore. Such tales were
made up by old women scared

to be thrust from the hearth,
shoved into the street to starve.
Who fears an old woman pushing
a grocery cart? She is talking

to god as she shuffles along,
her life in her pockets. You
are the true child of her heart
and you see living garbage.

Growing up haunted

When I enter through the hatch of memory
those claustrophobic chambers,
my adolescence in the booming fifties
of General Eisenhower, General Foods
and General Motors, I see our dreams
obsolescent mannequins in Dior frocks
armored, prefabricated bodies;
and I see our nightmares, powerful
as a wine red sky and wall of fire.

Fear was the underside of every leaf
we turned, the knowledge that our
cousins, our other selves, had been
starved and butchered to ghosts.
The question every smoggy morning
presented like a covered dish:
why are you living and all those
mirror selves, sisters, gone
into smoke like stolen cigarettes.

I remember my grandmother's cry
when she learned the death of all she
remembered, girls she bathed with,
young men with whom she shyly
flirted, wooden shul where
her father rocked and prayed,
red haired aunt plucking the
balalaika, world of sun and snow
turned to shadows on a yellow page.

Assume no future you may not have
to fight for, to die for, muttered
ghosts gathered on the foot
of my bed each night. What you
carry in your blood is us,
the books we did not write,
music we could not make, a world
gone from gristle to smoke, only
as real now as words can make it.

At the well

Though I'm blind now and age
has gutted me to rubbing bones
knotted up in a leather sack
like Old Man Jacob I wrestled an angel.
It happened near that well by Peniel
where the water runs copper cold
even in drought. Sore and dusty
I was traveling my usual rounds
wary of strangers—for some men
think nothing of setting on any woman
alone—doctoring a bit, setting bones,
herbs and simples I know well,
divining for water with a switch,
selling my charms of odd shaped bones
and stones with fancy names to less
skeptical women wanting a lover, a son,
a husband, or relief from one.

The stones were sharp as shinbones under me.
When I awoke at midnight it had come,
a presence furious as a goat about to butt;
amused as those yellow eyes
sometimes seem just before
the hind legs kick hard.
The angel struck me
and we wrestled all that night.
My dust stained gristle of a body
clad in proper village black
was pushed against him
and his fiery chest
fell through me like a star.
Raw with bruises, with my muscles
sawing like donkey's brays,
I thought fighting can be like

making love. Then in the grey
placental dawn I saw.

"I know you now, face
on a tree of fire
eyes of my youngest sweetest
dead, face I saw in the mirror
right after my first child
was born—before it failed—
when I was beautiful.
Whatever you are
I've won a blessing from you."

The angel, "Yes, we have met
at doors thrust open to an empty room,
a garden, or a pit.
My gifts have human faces
hieroglyphs that command
you without yielding what they mean.
Cast yourself and I will bless your cast
till your bones are dice
for the wind to roll.
I am the demon of beginnings
for those who leap their thresholds
and let the doors swing shut."

My hair bristling, I stood.
"Get away from me, old
enemy. I know the lying
radiance of that face:
my lover I trusted as the fish
the water, who left me
carrying his child.
The man who bought me
with his strength and beat
me for his weakness.
The girl I saved who turned
and sold her skin
for an easy bed in a house
of slaves. The boy fresh
as a willow sapling
smashed on the stones of war."

"I am the spirit of hinges,
 the fever that lives in dice
 and cards, what is picked
up and thrown down. I am
the new that is ancient,
the hope that hurts,
what begins in what has ended.
Mine is the double vision
that everything is sacred, and trivial,
and I love the blue beetle
clicking in the grass as much
as you. Shall I bless you
child and crone?"

"What has plucked the glossy
pride of hair from my scalp,
loosened my teeth in their sockets
wrung my breasts dry as gullies,
rubbed ashes into my sleep
but chasing you?
Now I clutch a crust and I hold on.
Get from me
wielder of the heart's mirages.
I will follow you to no more graves."
I spat
and she gathered her tall shuddering wings
and scaled the streaks of dawn
a hawk on fire soaring
and I stood there and could hear the water
burbling and raised my hand
before my face and groped:
What has the sun gone out?
Why is it dark?

For each age, its amulet

Each illness has its demon, burning you with
its fever, beating its quick wings.
Do not leave an infant alone in the house,
my grandmother said, for Lilith is hovering,
hungry. Avoid sleeping in a new house alone.
Demons come to death as flies do, hanging
on the sour sweetish wind. Protect yourself
in an unclean place by spitting three times.
A pregnant woman must go to bed with a knife.
Put iron in a hen's nest to keep it laying.
Demons suck eggs and squeeze the breath from chicks.
Circle yourself with salt and pray.

By building containers of plutonium
with the power to kill for longer than humans
have walked upright, demons are driven off.
Demons lurk in dark skins, white skins,
demons speak another language, have funny hair.
Very fast planes that fall from the sky
regularly like ostriches trying to fly, protect.
Best of all is the burning of money ritually
in the pentagon shaped shrine. In Langley
the largest prayer wheel computer recites spells
composed of all words written, spoken, thought
taped and stolen from every person alive.

Returning to the cemetery in the old Prague ghetto

Like bad teeth jammed crooked in a mouth
I think, no, because it goes on and on,
rippling in uneven hillocks among the linden
trees drooping, their papery leaves piling
up in the narrow paths that thread
between the crowded tilting slabs.

Stone pages the wind blew open.
The wind petrified into individual
cries. Prisoners penned together
with barely room to stand upright.
Souls of the dead Jews of Prague
waiting for justice under the acid rain.

So much and no further shall you go,
your contaminated dead confined between
strait walls like the ghetto itself.
So what to do? Every couple of generations,
pile on the dirt, raise the stones up
and add another layer of fresh bones.

The image I circle and do not want:
naked pallid bodies whipped through
the snow and driven into the chamber,
so crowded that dying slowly in the poison
cloud they could not fall as their nerves
burned slowly black, upright in death.

In my luggage I carried from Newcomb Hollow
two stones for Rabbi Loew's memorial
shaped like a narrow tent, one for Judah
on his side and one for Perl on hers.
But my real gift is the novel they
speak through. For David Gans, astronomer,

geographer, historian, insatiably curious
and neat as a cat in his queries,
I brought a fossil to lay at the foot
of his grave marked with a goose and a star,
Mogen David, so the illiterate could find
him, as Judah has his rampant lion.

In '68 I had to be hoisted
over the fence. Among the stones
I was alone except for a stray black cat
that sang to me incessantly of need,
so hungry it ate bread from my jacket pocket.
This year buses belch out German tourists

and the graves are well tended.
This is a place history clutches you
by the foot as you walk the human earth,
like a hand grabbing from the grave,
not to frighten but to admonish.
Remember. History is the iron

in your blood carrying oxygen
so you can burn food and live.
Read this carved book with your fingers
and your failing eyes. The language
will speak in you silently
nights afterward, stone and bone.

The fundamental truth

The Christian right, Islamic Jihad,
the Jewish right bank settlers bringing
the Messiah down, the Japanese sects
who worship by bombing subways,
they all hate each other
but more they hate the mundane,
ordinary people who love living
more than dying in radiant glory,
who shuffle and sigh and make supper.

They need a planet of their own,
perhaps even a barren moon
with artificial atmosphere,
where they will surely be nearer
to their gods and their fiercest
enemies, where they can kill
to their heart's peace
kill to the last standing man
and leave the rest of us be.

Not mystics to whom the holy
comes in the core of struggle
in a shimmer of blinding quiet,
not scholars haggling out the inner
meaning of gnarly ancient sentences.
No, the holy comes to these zealots
as a license to kill, for self doubt
and humility have dried like mud
under their marching feet.

They have far more in common
with each other, these braggarts
of hatred, the iron hearted
in whose ear a voice spoke
once and left them deaf.
Their faith is founded on death
of others, and everyone is other
to them, whose Torah, Bible and Koran
are splattered in letters of blood.

Amidah: on our feet we speak to you

We rise to speak
a web of bodies aligned like notes of music.

I.

Bless what brought us through
the sea and the fire; we are caught
in history like whales in polar ice.
Yet you have taught us to push against the walls,

to reach out and pull each other along,
to strive to find the way through
if there is no way around, to go on.
To utter ourselves with every breath

against the constriction of fear,
to know ourselves as the body born from Abraham
and Sarah, born out of rock and desert.
We reach back through two hundred arches of hips

long dust, carrying their memories inside us
to live again in our life, Issac and Rebecca,
Rachel, Jacob, Leah. We say words shaped
by ancient use like steps worn into rock.

2.

Bless the quiet of sleep
easing over the ravaged body, that quiets
the troubled waters of the mind to a pool
in which shines the placid broad face of the moon.

Bless the teaching of how to open
in love so all the doors and windows of the body
swing wide on their rusty hinges
and we give ourselves with both hands.

Bless what stirs in us compassion
for the hunger of the chickadee in the storm
starving for seeds we can carry out,
the wounded cat wailing in the alley,

that shows us our face in a stranger,
that teaches us what we clutch shrivels

but what we give goes off in the world
carrying bread to people not yet born.

Bless the gift of memory
that breaks unbidden, released
from a flower or a cup of tea
so the dead move like rain through the room.

Bless what forces us to invent
goodness every morning and what never frees
us from the cost of knowledge, which is
to act on what we know again and again.

3.

All living are one and holy, let us remember
as we eat, as we work, as we walk and drive.
All living are one and holy, we must make ourselves worthy.
We must act out justice and mercy and healing
as the sun rises and as the sun sets,
as the moon rises and the stars wheel above us,
we must repair goodness.
We must praise the power of the one that joins us.
Whether we plunge in or thrust ourselves far out
finally we reach the face of glory too bright
for our eyes and yet we burn and we give light.

We will try to be holy,
we will try to repair the world given us to hand on.
Precious is this treasure of words and knowledge and deeds
that moves inside us.
Holy is the hand that works for peace and for justice,
holy is the mouth that speaks for goodness
holy is the foot that walks toward mercy.

Let us lift each other on our shoulders and carry each other along.
Let holiness move in us.
Let us pay attention to its small voice.
Let us see the light in others and honor that light.
Remember the dead who paid our way here dearly, dearly
and remember the unborn for whom we build our houses.

Praise the light that shines before us, through us, after us,
Amein.

Kaddish

Look around us, search above us, below, behind.
We stand in a great web of being joined together.
Let us praise, let us love the life we are lent
passing through us in the body of Israel
and our own bodies, let's say amein.

Time flows through us like water.
The past and the dead speak through us.
We breathe out our children's children, blessing.

Blessed is the earth from which we grow,
Blessed the life we are lent,
blessed the ones who teach us,
blessed the ones we teach,
blessed is the word that cannot say the glory
that shines through us and remains to shine
flowing past distant suns on the way to forever.
Let's say amein.

Blessed is light, blessed is darkness,
but blessed above all else is peace
which bears the fruits of knowledge
on strong branches, let's say amein.

Peace that bears joy into the world,
peace that enables love, peace over Israel
everywhere, blessed and holy is peace, let's say amein.

Wellfleet Shabbat

The hawk eye of the sun slowly shuts.
The breast of the bay is softly feathered
dove grey. The sky is barred like the sand
when the tide trickles out.

The great doors of Shabbat are swinging
open over the ocean, loosing the moon
floating up slow distorted vast, a copper
balloon just sailing free.

The wind slides over the waves, patting
them with its giant hand, and the sea
stretches its muscles in the deep,
purrs and rolls over.

The sweet beeswax candles flicker
and sigh, standing between the phlox
and the roast chicken. The wine shines
its red lantern of joy.

Here on this piney sandspit, the Shekinah
comes on the short strong wings of the seaside
sparrow raising her song and bringing
down the fresh clean night.

The head of the year

The moon is dark tonight, a new
moon for a new year. It is
hollow and hungers to be full.
It is the black zero of beginning.

Now you must void yourself
of injuries, insults, incursions.
Go with empty hands to those
you have hurt and make amends.

It is not too late. It is early
and about to grow. Now
is the time to do what you
know you must and have feared

to begin. Your face is dark
too as you turn inward to face
yourself, the hidden twin
of all you must grow to be.

Forgive the dead year. Forgive
yourself. What will be wants
to push through your fingers.
The light you seek hides

in your belly. The light you
crave longs to stream from
your eyes. You are the moon
that will wax in new goodness.

Breadcrumbs

Some time on Rosh Hashana I go,
a time dictated by tide charts,
services. The once I did tashlich

on the rising tide and the crumbs
came back to me, my energy soured,
vinegar of anxiety. Now I eye the times.

I choose the dike, where the Herring River
pours in and out of the bay, where at
low tide in September blue herons stalk

totemic to spear the alewives hastening
silver-sided from the fresh ponds to
the sea. As I toss my crumbs, muttering

prayers, a fisherman rebukes me: It's
not right to feed the fish, it distracts
them from his bait. Sometimes it's

odd to be a Jew, like a three-
legged heron with bright purple head,
an ibis in white plumes diving

except that with global warming
we do sometimes glimpse an ibis
in our marshes, and I am rooted here

to abide the winter when this tourist
has gone back to Cincinnati.
My rituals are mated to this fawn

colored land floating on the horizon
of water. My havurah calls itself
Am haYam, people of the sea,

and we are wedded to the oceans
as truly as the Venetian doge who tossed
his gold ring to the Adriatic.

All rivers flow at last into the sea
but here it is, at once. So we stand
the tourist casting for his fish

and I tossing my bread. The fish
snap it up at once. Tonight perhaps
he will broil my sins for supper.

The New Year of the Trees

It is the New Year of the Trees, but here
the ground is frozen under the crust of snow.
The trees snooze, their buds tight as nuts.
Rhododendron leaves roll up their stiff scrolls.

In the white and green north of the diaspora
I am stirred by a season that will not arrive
for six weeks, as wines on far continents prickle
to bubbles when their native vines bloom.

What blossoms here are birds jostling
at feeders, pecking sunflower seeds
and millet through the snow: tulip red
cardinal, daffodil finch, larkspur jay,

the pansybed of sparrows and juncos, all hungry.
They too are planters of trees, spreading seeds
of favorites along fences. On the earth closed
to us all as a book in a language we cannot

yet read, the seeds, the bulbs, the eggs
of the fervid green year await release.
Over them on February's cold table I spread
a feast. Wings rustle like summer leaves.

Charoset

Sweet and sticky
I always make too much
at Pesach so I have
an excuse to eat you
all week.

Moist and red
the female treat
nothing at all like clay
for bricks, nothing
like mortar.

No, you are sweet as
a mouth kissing,
you are fragrant
with cinnamon
spicy as havdalah boxes.

Don't go on too long,
you whisper sweetly.
Heed the children
growing restive, their
bellies growling.

You speak of pleasure
in the midst of remembered pain.
You offer the first taste
of the meal, promising joy
like a picnic on a stone

where long ago an ancestor
was buried, too long
ago to weep. We nod
and remembering is enough
to offer, like honey.

If much of what we must
recall is bitter, you
are the reminder that
joy too lights its candles
tonight in the mind.

Lamb Shank: Z'roah

It grosses out many of my friends.
They don't eat meat, let alone
place it on a ritual platter.
I am not so particular, or more so.

Made of flesh and bone, liver
and sinew, salty blood and brain,
I know they weren't ghosts who trekked
out of baked mud huts into the desert.

Blood was spilled, red and real:
first ours, then theirs. Blood
splashed on the doorposts proclaimed
in danger the rebellion within.

We are pack and herd animals.
One Jew is not a Jew, but we are
a people together, plural, joined.
We were made flesh and we bled.

And we fled, under the sign
of the slaughtered lamb to live
and die for each other. We are
meat that thinks and sings.

Matzoh

Flat you are as a doormat
and as homely.
No crust, no glaze, you lack
a cosmetic glow.
You break with a snap.
You are dry as a twig
split from an oak
in midwinter.
You are bumpy as a mud basin
in a drought.
Square as a slab of pavement,
you have no inside
to hide raisins or seeds.
You are pale as the full moon
pocked with craters.

What we see is what we get,
honest, plain, dry
shining with nostalgia
as if baked with light
instead of heat.
The bread of flight and haste
in the mouth you
promise, home.

Maggid

The courage to let go of the door, the handle.
The courage to shed the familiar walls whose very
stains and leaks are comfortable as the little moles
of the upper arm; stains that recall a feast,
a child's naughtiness, a loud blattering storm
that slapped the roof hard, pouring through.

The courage to abandon the graves dug into the hill,
the small bones of children and the brittle bones
of the old whose marrow hunger had stolen;
the courage to desert the tree planted and only
begun to bear; the riverside where promises were
shaped; the street where their empty pots were broken.

The courage to leave the place whose language you learned
as early as your own, whose customs however dan-
gerous or demeaning, bind you like a halter
you have learned to pull inside, to move your load;
the land fertile with the blood spilled on it;
the roads mapped and annotated for survival.

The courage to walk out of the pain that is known
into the pain that cannot be imagined,
mapless, walking into the wilderness, going
barefoot with a canteen into the desert;
stuffed in the stinking hold of a rotting ship;
sailing off the map into dragons' mouths,

Cathay, India, Siberia, goldeneh medina,
leaving bodies by the way like abandoned treasure.
So they walked out of Egypt. So they bribed their way

out of Russia under loads of straw; so they steamed
out of the bloody smoking charnelhouse of Europe
on overloaded freighters forbidden all ports—

out of pain into death or freedom or a different
painful dignity, into squalor and politics.
We Jews are all born of wanderers, with shoes
under our pillows and a memory of blood that is ours
raining down. We honor only those Jews who changed
tonight, those who chose the desert over bondage

who walked into the strange and became strangers
and gave birth to children who could look down
on them standing on their shoulders for having
been slaves. We honor those who let go of every-
thing but freedom, who ran, who revolted, who fought,
who became other by saving themselves.

Coming up on September

White butterflies, with single
black fingerpaint eyes on their wings
dart and settle, eddy and mate
over the green tangle of vines
in Labor Day morning steam.

The year grinds into ripeness
and rot, grapes darkening,
pears yellowing, the first
Virginia creeper twining crimson,
the grasses, dry straw to burn.

The New Year rises, beckoning
across the umbrellas on the sand.
I begin to reconsider my life.
What is the yield of my impatience?
What is the fruit of my resolve?

Now is the time to let the mind
search backward like the raven loosed
to see what can feed us. Now,
the time to cast the mind forward
to chart an aerial map of the months.

The New Year is a great door
that stands across the evening and Yom
Kippur is the second door. Between them
are song and silence, stone and clay pot
to be filled from within myself.

I will find there both ripeness and rot,
what I have done and undone,
what I must let go with the waning days
and what I must take in. With the last
tomatoes, we harvest the fruit of our lives.

Nishmat

When night slides under with the last dimming star
and the red sky lightens between the trees,
and the heron glides tipping heavy wings in the river,
when crows stir and cry out their harsh joy,
and swift creatures of the night run toward their burrows,
and the deer raises her head and sniffs the freshening air,
and the shadows grow more distinct and then shorten,

then we rise into the day still clean as new snow.
The cat washes its paw and greets the day with gratitude.
Leviathan salutes breaching with a column of steam.
The hawk turning in the sky cries out a prayer like a knife.
We must wonder at the sky now thin as a speckled eggshell,
that now piles up its boulders of storm to crash down,
that now hangs a furry grey belly into the street.

Every day we find a new sky and a new earth
with which we are trusted like a perfect toy.
We are given the salty river of our blood
winding through us, to remember the sea and our
kindred under the waves, the hot pulsing that knocks
in our throats to consider our cousins in the grass
and the trees, all bright scattered rivulets of life.

We are given the wind within us, the breath
to shape into words that steal time, that touch
like hands and pierce like bullets, that waken
truth and deceit, sorrow and pity and joy,
that waste precious air in complaints, in lies,
in floating traps for power on the dirty air.
Yet holy breath still stretches our lungs to sing.

We are given the body, that momentary kibbutz
of elements that have belonged to frog and polar
bear, corn and oak tree, volcano and glacier.
We are lent for a time these minerals in water
and a morning every day, a morning to wake up,
rejoice and praise life in our spines, our throats,
our knees, our genitals, our brains, our tongues.

We are given fire to see against the dark,
to think, to read, to study how we are to live,
to bank in ourselves against defeat and despair
that cool and muddy our resolves, that make us forget
what we saw we must do. We are given passion
to rise like the sun in our minds with the new day
and burn the debris of habit and greed and fear.

We stand in the midst of the burning world
primed to burn with compassionate love and justice,
to turn inward and find holy fire at the core,
to turn outward and see the world that is all
of one flesh with us, see under the trash,
through the smog, the furry bee in the apple blossom,
the trout leaping, the candles our ancestors lit for us.

Fill us as the tide rustles into the reeds in the marsh.
Fill us as rushing water overflows the pitcher.
Fill us as light fills a room with its dancing.
Let the little quarrels of the bones and the snarling
of the lesser appetites and the whining of the ego cease.
Let silence still us so you may show us your shining
and we can out of that stillness rise and praise.

from
Colors Passing Through Us

No one came home

1.

Max was in bed that morning, pressed
against my feet, walking to my pillow
to kiss my nose, long and lean with aqua-
marine eyes, my sun prince who thought

himself my lover. He was cream and golden
orange, strong willed, lord of the other
cats and his domain. He lay on my chest
staring into my eyes. He went out at noon.

He never came back. A smear of blood
on the grass at the side of the road
where we saw a huge coywolf the next
evening. We knew he had been eaten

yet we could not know. We kept looking
for him, calling him, searching. He
vanished from our lives in an hour. My cats
have always died in old age, slowly

with abundant warning. Not Max.
He left a hole in my waking.

2.

A woman leaves her children in day care,
goes off to her secretarial job
on the 100th floor, conscientious always
to arrive early, because she needs the money

for her children, for health insurance,
for rent and food and clothing and fees
for all the things kids need, whose father
has two new children and a great lawyer.

They are going to eat chicken that night
she has promised, and the kids talk of that
together, fried chicken with adobo, rice
and black beans, food rich as her love.

The day is bright as a clean mirror.

3.

His wife has morning sickness so does
not rise for breakfast. He stops for coffee,
a yogurt, rushing for the 8:08 train.
Ignoring the window, he writes his five

pages, the novel that is going to make
him famous, cut him loose from the desk
where he is chained to the phone
eight to ten hours, making cold calls.

In his head, naval battles rage. He
has been studying Midway, the Coral
Sea, Guadalcanal. He can recite
tonnage, tides, the problems with torpedoes.

For five years, he has prepared.
His makeshift office in the basement
is lined with books and maps. His book
will sing with bravery and error.

The day is blue and whistles like a robin.

4.

His father was a fireman and his brother.
He once imagined being a rapper
but by the end of high school, he knew
it was his calling, it was his family way.

As there are trapeze families, clans
who perform with tigers or horses,
the Irish travelers, tinkers, Gypsies,
those born to work the earth of their farm,

and those who inherit vast fortunes
built of the bones of others, so families
inherit danger and grace, the pursuit
of the safety of others before their own.

The morning smelled of the river,
of doughnuts, of coffee, of leaves.

5.

When a man fell into the molten steel
the company would deliver an ingot
to bury. Something. Where I live
on the Cape, lost at sea means no body.

You can't bury a coffin length of sea
water. There are stones in our grave
yards with lists of names, the sailors
from ships gone down in a storm.

MIA means no body, no answer,
hope that is hopeless, the door
that can never be quite closed.
Lives are broken off like tree limbs

in a storm. Other lives simply dissolve
like salt in warm water and there is
no shadow on the pavement, no trace.
They puff into nothing. We can't believe.

We die still expecting an answer.

6.

Los desparecidos. Did we notice?
Did we care? In Chile, funded,
assisted by the CIA, a democratic
government was torn down and thousands

brought into a stadium and never seen
again. Reports of torture, reports of graves
in the mountains, bodies dumped at sea
reports of your wife, your son, your

father arrested and then vanished
like cigarette smoke, gone like
a whisper you aren't quite sure you
heard, a living person who must, who

must be somewhere, anywhere, lost,
wounded, boxed in a cell, in exile,

under a stone, somewhere, bones,
a skull, a button, a wisp of cloth.

In Argentina, the women marched
for those who had disappeared.
Did we notice? That happened
in those places, those other places

where people don't speak English,
eat strange spicy foods, have dictators
or Communists or sambas or goas.
They didn't count. We didn't count

them or those they said had been
there alive and now who knew?
Not us. The terror has come home.
Will it make us better or worse?

7.

When will we understand what terrorists
never believe, that we are all
precious in our loving, all tender
in our flesh and webbed together?

That no one should be torn
out of the fabric of friends and family,
the sweet and sour work of loving,
burnt anonymously, carelessly

because of nothing they ever did
because of hatred they never knew
because of nobody they ever touched
or left untouched, turned suddenly

to dust on a perfect September
morning bright as a new apple
when nothing they did would
ever again make any difference.

Photograph of my mother sitting on the steps

My mother who isn't anyone's
just her own intact and yearning
self complete as a birch tree
sits on the tenement steps.

She is awkwardly lovely, her face
pure as a single trill perfectly
prolonged on a violin, yet she
knows the camera sees her

and she arranges her body
like a flower in a vase to be
displayed, admired she hopes.
She longs to be luminous

and visible, to shine in the eyes
of it must be a handsome man,
who will carry her away—and he
will into poverty and an abortion

but not yet. Now she drapes
her best, her only good dress
inherited from her sister who dances
on the stage, around her legs

that she does not like
and leans a little forward
because she does like her breasts.
How she wants love to bathe

her in honeyed light lifting her
up through smoky clouds clamped
on the Pittsburgh slum. Blessed
are we who cannot know

what will come to us,
our upturned faces following
through the sky
the sun of love.

One reason I like opera

In movies, you can tell the heroine
because she is blonder and thinner
than her sidekick. The villainess
is darkest. If a woman is fat,
she is a joke and will probably die.

In movies, the blondest are the best
and in bleaching lies not only purity
but victory. If two people are both
extra pretty, they will end up
in the final clinch.

Only the flawless in face and body
win. That is why I treat
movies as less interesting
than comic books. The camera
is stupid. It sucks surfaces.

Let's go to the opera instead.
The heroine is fifty and weighs
as much as a '65 Chevy with fins.
She could crack your jaw in her fist.
She can hit high C lying down.

The tenor the women scream for
wolfs an eight course meal daily.
He resembles a bull on hind legs.
His thighs are the size of beer kegs.
His chest is a redwood with hair.

Their voices twine, golden serpents.
Their voices rise like the best
fireworks and hang and hang
then drift slowly down descending
in brilliant and still fiery sparks.

The hippopotamus baritone (the villain)
has a voice that could give you
an orgasm right in your seat.
His voice smokes with passion.
He is hot as lava. He erupts nightly.

The contralto is, however, svelte.
She is supposed to be the soprano's
mother, but is ten years younger,
beautiful and Black. Nobody cares.
She sings you into her womb where you rock.

What you see is work like digging a ditch,
hard physical labor. What you hear
is magic as tricky as knife throwing.
What you see is strength like any
great athlete's; what you hear

is skill rendered precisely as the best
Swiss watchmaker. The body is
resonance. The body is the cello case.
The body just is. The voice loud
as hunger remagnetizes your bones.

My mother gives me her recipe

Take some flour. Oh, I don't know,
like two–three cups, and you cut
in the butter. Now some women
they make it with shortening.
but I say butter, even though
that meant you had to have fish, see?

You cut up some apples. Not those
stupid sweet ones. Apples for the cake,
they have to have some bite, you know?
A little sour in the sweet, like love.
You slice them into little moons.
No, no! Like half or crescent
moons. You aren't listening.

You mix sugar and cinnamon and cloves,
some women use allspice. You coat
every little moon. Did I say you add
milk? Oh, just till it feels right.
Use your hands. Milk in the cake part!

Then you pat it into a pan, I like
round ones, but who cares?
I forgot to say you add baking powder.
Did I forget a little lemon on the apples?
Then you just bake it. Well, till it's done
of course. Did I remember you place
the apples in rows? You can make
a pattern, like a weave. It's pretty
that way. I like things pretty.

It's just a simple cake.
Any fool can make it
except your aunt. I
gave her the recipe
but she never
got it right.

The good old days at home sweet home

On Monday my mother washed.
It was the way of the world,
all those lines of sheets flapping
in the narrow yards of the neighborhood,
the pulleys stretching out second
and third floor windows.

Down in the dank steamy basement,
washtubs vast and grey, the wringer
sliding between the washer
and each tub. At least every
year she or I caught
a hand in it.

Tuesday my mother ironed.
One iron was the mangle.
She sat at it feeding in towels,
sheets, pillowcases.
The hand ironing began
with my father's underwear.

She ironed his shorts.
She ironed his socks.
She ironed his undershirts.
Then came the shirts
a half hour to each, the starch
boiling on the stove.

I forget blueing. I forget
the props that held up the line
clattering down. I forget

chasing the pigeons that shat
on her billowing housedresses.
I forget clothespins in the teeth.

Tuesday my mother ironed my
father's underwear. Wednesday
she mended, darned socks on
a wooden egg. Shined shoes.
Thursday she scrubbed floors.
Put down newspapers to keep

them clean. Friday she
vacuumed, dusted, polished,
scraped, waxed, pummeled.
How did you become a feminist
interviewers always ask
as if to say, when did this

rare virus attack your brain?
It could have been Sunday
when she washed the windows,
Thursday when she burned
the trash, bought groceries
hauling the heavy bags home.

It could have been any day
she did again and again what
time and dust obliterated
at once until stroke broke
her open. I think it was Tuesday
when she ironed my father's shorts.

The day my mother died

I seldom have premonitions of death.
That day opened like any
ordinary can of tomatoes.

The alarm drilled into my ear.
The cats stirred and one leapt off.
The scent of coffee slipped into my head

like a lover into my arms and I sighed,
drew the curtains and examined
the face of the day.

I remember no dreams of loss.
No dark angel rustled ominous wings
or whispered gravely.

I was caught by surprise
like the trout that takes the fly
and I gasped in the fatal air.

You were gone suddenly as a sound
fading in the coil of the ear
no trace, no print, no ash

just the emptiness of stilled air.
My hunger feeds on itself.
My hands are stretched out

to grasp and find only their
own weight bearing them down
toward the dark cold earth.

Love has certain limited powers

The dead walk with us briefly,
suddenly just behind on the narrow
path like a part in the hairy grass.
We feel them between our shoulder
blades and we can speak, but if
we turn, like Eurydice they're gone.

The dead lie with us briefly
swimming through the warm salty
pool of darkness flat as flounders,
floating like feathers on the shafts
of silver moonlight. Their hair
brushes our face and is gone.

The dead speak to us through
the scent of red musk roses,
through steam rising from green tea,
through the spring rain scratching
on the pane. If I try to recapture
your voice, silence grates

in my ears, the mocking rush
of silence. But months later
I stand at the stove stirring a pot
of soup and you say, *Too much salt,*
and you say, *You have my hair,*
and, *Pain wears out like anything else.*

Little lights

Tonight I light the first candle
on the chanukiyah by the window
and then a second in the bathtub,
the yahrzeit candle for your death.

I am always sad the first night
of a holiday when we should rejoice.
This night nineteen years ago
the light of your mind snuffed out.

The Chanukkah candles burn quickly
two hours and they gutter out
their short time burnt up.
We did not know how old you were—

you'd always fudged your age,
you had no birth certificate—
I don't know if you knew
your birth date and place, for real.

Grandma always gave a different
answer and then shrugged. Your
mother is younger than me and
older than you, what else matters?

Yes, there's Moses and David,
Babylon and the Talmud,
Maimonides, and then we appear
out of a cloud of smoke and haze

of old blood there among the Jew-
haters clutching a few bundles.
My people poor, without names,
histories vanished into the hard soil

but we had stories with pedigrees:
my female ancestors told them,

Lilith, the golem, Rabbi Nachman,
the Maccabees, all simultaneous

all swarming around my bed
all caught in my hair as you
washed it with tar soap, relating
fables, family gossip, bubele

maisehs, precious handed down
the true family jewels, my dowry.
Those little flames you lit in my
mind burn on paper for you,

your true yahrzeit, all year
every year of my aging life.

Gifts that keep on giving

You know when you unwrap them:
fruitcake is notorious. There were only
51 of them baked in 1917 by the
personal chef of Rasputin. The mad monk
ate one. That was what finally killed him

But there are many more bouncers:
bowls green and purple spotted like lepers.
Vases of inept majolica in the shape
of wheezing frogs or overweight lilies.
Sweaters sized for Notre Dame's hunchback.

Hourglasses of no use humans
can devise. Gloves to fit three-toed sloths.
Mufflers of screaming plaid acrylic.
Necklaces and pins that transform
any outfit to a thrift shop reject.

Boxes of candy so stale and sticky
the bonbons pull teeth faster than
your dentist. Weird sauces bought
at warehouse sales no one will ever
taste unless suicidal or blind.

Immortal as vampires, these gifts
circulate from birthdays to Christmas,
from weddings to anniversaries.
Even if you send them to the dump,
they resurface, bobbing up on the third

day like the corpses they call floaters.
After all living have turned to dust
and ashes, in the ruins of cities
alien archeologists will judge our
civilization by these monstrous relics.

The yellow light

When I see—obsolete, forgotten—
a yellow porchlight, I am transported
to muggy Michigan evenings.
The air is thick with July.

We are playing pinochle.
Every face card is a relative.
Now we are playing Hearts
but I am the Queen of Spades.

Mosquitoes hum over the weedy
lake. An owl groans in the pines.
Moths hurl themselves against
the screens, a dry brown rain.

Yellow makes every card black.
The eyes of my uncles are avid.
They are playing for pennies
and blood. One shows off

a new Buick, one a new wife.
The women are whispering
about bellies and beds.
It always smells like fried perch.

I am afraid I will never grow up.
I think the owl is calling me
over the black water to hide
in the pines and turn, turn

into something strange and dark
with wings and talons and words
of a more powerful language
than uncles and aunts know,
than uncles and aunts understand.

The new era, c. 1946

It was right after the war of my childhood
World War II, and the parks were wide open.
The lights were all turned on, house
lights, streetlights, neon like green
and purple blood pumping the city's heart.
I had grown up in brownout, blackout,
my father the air raid warden going
house to house to check that no pencil
of light stabbed out between blackout curtains.
Now it was summer and Detroit was celebrating.

Fireworks burst open their incandescent petals
flaring in arcs down into my wide eyes.
A band was playing "Stars and Stripes Forever."
Then the lights came on brighter and starker
than day and sprayers began to mist the field.
It was the new miracle DDT in which we danced
its faint perfumy smell like privet along the sidewalks.
It was comfort in mist, for there would be no more
mosquitoes forever, and we would always be safe.

Out in Nevada soldiers were bathing in fallout.
People downwind of the tests were drinking
heavy water out of their faucets. Cancer
was the rising sign in the neon painted night.
Little birds fell out of the trees but no one

noticed. We had so many birds then.
In Europe American cigarettes were money.
Here all the kids smoked on street corners.
I used to light kitchen matches with my thumbnail.

My parents threw out their Depression ware
and bought Melmac plastic dishes.
They believed in plastic and the promise
that when they got old, they would go
to Florida and live like the middle class.
My brother settled in California with a new
wife and his old discontent. New car,
new refrigerator, Mama and Daddy have new hats.
Crouch and cover. Ashes, all fall down.

Winter promises

Tomatoes rosy as perfect babies' buttocks,
eggplants glossy as waxed fenders,
purple neon flawless glistening
peppers, pole beans fecund and fast
growing as Jack's Viagra-sped stalk,
big as truck tire zinnias that mildew
will never wilt, roses weighing down
a bush never touched by black spot,
brave little fruit trees shouldering up
their spotless ornaments of glass fruit:

I lie on the couch under a blanket
of seed catalogs ordering far
too much. Sleet slides down
the windows, a wind edged
with ice knifes through every crack.
Lie to me, sweet garden-mongers:
I want to believe every promise,
to trust in five pound tomatoes
and dahlias brighter than the sun
that was eaten by frost last week.

The gardener's litany

We plant, it is true.
I start the tiny seedlings
in peat pots, water, feed.

But the garden is alive
in the night with its own
adventures. Slugs steal

out, snails carry their
spiraled houses upward,
rabbits hop over the fence.

The garden like a green
and bronze goddess loves
zucchini this year but will

not give us cucumbers.
She does as she pleases.
Purple beans but no yellows.

Serve me, she whispers,
maybe I will give you tomatoes,
or maybe I will hatch into

thousands of green caterpillars
maybe I will grow only bindweed,
joe-pye weed and dandelions.

All gardeners worship weather
and luck. We begin in compost
and end in decay. The life

of one is the death of the other.
Beetles eat squash plant. Bird
eats beetle. Soil eats all.

Eclipse at the solstice

New moon and the hottest sun:
It should be the day of the triumphant
sun marching like a red elephant
up the lapis arch of sky.

The moon is invisible, shy,
almost wounded. She draws
the thin short darkness around her
like a torn dress.

Then in the fat of the afternoon
she slides over the sun
enveloping him. I have
conquered, she croons,

brought darkness and put the birds
to sleep, raised the twilight wind.
But then his corona shines
around her and she sees.

You really are a lion with mane
of white fire, you beauty. So
she gives him the day back,
slowly, and lets him roar.

The rain as wine

It is a ripe rain
coming down in big fat drops
like grapes dropping on the roof—
white grapes round as moons.

It is coming in waves
whooshing through the trees.
Silvery, intimate, it softens
and washes the parched air.

It falls on my face
like a blessing.
It sweetens my body
rolling down my upstretched arms.

The rain blesses us
as it opens the cracked earth
as it opens us to itself:
the sweet gush of August rain.

Taconic at midnight

At eleven we headed home, north
on the Taconic Parkway to the Mass Pike,
a mild late September night with fog
drifting in great hanks like white Spanish
moss, wavering in translucent
banners across the narrow highway,
diffusing moonlight, deflecting our beams.

Almost at once we began to see them:
deer congregated on each side where
the woods opened, dozens in a clearing,
bucks in the road, does milling about.
We drove slower and slower, inching
past, steering among them who ignored
our intrusion. They were intent

on each other, for this gathering
was a mating mart like a mixer:
but they were serious, examining
each other with desperate attention,
an air of silky sexy tension roiling
like the fog that sank and lifted
bedazzling their sleek flanks,

their shaking antlers. The road
did not belong. It should have been
rolled up like a bale of wire and stowed,
for this was a night of the ancient gods
when America floated on the turtle's back
and all things were still pristine
as the lucent brown eye of a virgin doe.

The equinox rush

The swan heads south in the night sky.
Overhead, the sharp white triangle
of Altair, Deneb and Vega prickles.
At dawn there is a hint of frost,
only etched on the truck down
at the foot of the drive.

A sharp shinned hawk eyes
chickadees at the feeder, swoops.
That afternoon over High Head
I see two more hawks passing
missile lean, hurrying before
a wind I cannot feel.

Everything quickens. Squirrels
rush to feed. Monarchs among
the milkweed raggedly zigzag
toward South America. Too early
for the final harvest, too early
to mulch and protect, too soon

to take off the screens, still
some sharp corner has been turned.
I am stirred to finish something.
A hint of cold frames the moment
and compresses it. Urgency
is the drug of the day.

Find a task and do it, the red
of the Virginia creeper warns.
The sunset is a brushfire.
I am hurrying, I am running hard
toward I don't know what,
but I mean to arrive before dark.

Seder with comet

The comet was still hanging in the sky
that year at Pesach, and of course
the full moon, as every year.

After the bulk of the seder, after
the long rich redolent meal, we all
went out on the road walking away

from the house whose lights we had
dimmed. There on the velvet playing
field of night we saw the moon rolling

toward us like a limestone millwheel
the whole sky pouring to fill our heads
a little drunk with the sweet wine

so that the stars sank in with a whisper
like a havdalah candle doused in wine
giving a little electric buzz to the brain.

Then we saw it, the comet like the mane
of a white lion, something holy to mark
this one more Passover with all of us

together, my old commune mates, friends
from here and the city, children I have known
since birth, all standing with our faces turned

up like pale sunflowers to the icy fire.
Then we went back to the house, drank
the last cup and sang till we were hoarse.

The cameo

My only time in Naples
the day we went to Pompeii
street sellers had them: big fine cameos
just like the one my grandma
left to me, a brooch. Seeing them

was finding a footprint in the street:
her small feet like my mother's
had passed here with her great
sophisticated love. Her rabbi
father married them on his deathbed.

They left Russia under a load of straw
a price on his head, no papers.
In Naples he sold his gold
watch to buy them passports
taking the name Bunin, after

the writer he admired.
What will you do in America?
the anarchist seller asked.
Make a revolution, he declaimed.
So he got a good price.

Off to Ellis Island, where the
immigration inspector added
an extra n and let them slip
in, Grandma secretly pregnant
under her too big black dress.

She insisted on mourning her father
though her husband objected.
But she kept her long chestnut
hair against custom, to please
him, who said such glory should

never be sacrificed, and any angels
tempted would have to come through
him. She did not know yet
he would be unfaithful, give her
eleven children to raise in squalor,

make no revolution but organize
unions, be killed by Pinkertons.
In Naples she danced through exotic
dangerous streets on his arm, proud
he could speak Italian and bargain

not only for passports cheap
but carved head and shoulders of a fine
looking woman he said resembled
her, and she was pleased although
already she did not believe him.

Miriam's cup

This cup of fresh water on the seder table at Pesach represents the well of Miriam, Moses' older sister who gave water to the children of Israel through the desert until her death. It compliments the traditional cup of Eliyahu.

The cup of Eliyahu holds wine;
the cup of Miriam holds water.
Wine is more precious
until you have no water.

Water that flows in our veins,
water that is the stuff of life
for we are made of breath
and water, vision

and fact. Eliyahu is
the extraordinary; Miriam
brings the daily wonders:
the joy of a fresh morning

like a newly prepared table,
a white linen cloth on which
nothing has yet spilled.
The descent into the heavy

waters of sleep healing us.
The scent of baking bread,
roasted chicken, fresh herbs,
the faces of friends across

the table. What sustains us
every morning, every evening,
the common miracles
like the taste of cool water.

Dignity

Near the end of your life you regard
me with a gaze clear and lucid
saying simply, I am, I will not be.

How foolish to imagine animals
don't comprehend death. Old
cats study it like a recalcitrant mouse.

You seek out warmth for your bones
close now to the sleek coat
that barely wraps them,

little knobs of spine, the jut
of hip bones, the skull
my fingers lightly caress.

Sometimes in the night you cry:
a deep piteous banner of gone
desire and current sorrow,

the fear that the night is long
and hungry and you pace
among its teeth feeling time

slipping through you cold and
slick. If I rise and fetch you back
to bed, you curl against me purring

able to grasp pleasure by the nape
even inside pain. Your austere
dying opens its rose of ash.

Old cat crying

The old cat stands on the flagstone
path through the herb garden,
crying, crying. She has what
the vet calls cognitive
dysfunction, as will we all
as will we all.

She is crying for the companion
who always came to her
from the time he drank
her milk, with whom she slept
four sharp ears from one
grey cushion of fur.

He should not have died
before her. She cries
for him to come. She
sniffed his body and knew
but she has forgotten
and he does not come.

I hold her and it is my
past I mourn, my mother,
lovers, friends whom
I shall never again summon
and the future's empty
silent rooms.

Traveling dream

I am packing to go to the airport
but somehow I am never packed.
I keep remembering more things
I keep forgetting.

Secretly the clock is bolting
forward ten minutes at a click
instead of one. Each time
I look away, it jumps.

Now I remember I have to find
the cats. I have five cats
even when I am asleep.
One is on the bed and I slip

her into the suitcase.
One is under the sofa. I
drag him out. But the tabby
in the suitcase has vanished.

Now my tickets have run away.
Maybe the cat has my tickets.
I can only find one cat.
My purse has gone into hiding.

Now it is time to get packed.
I take the suitcase down.
There is a cat in it but no clothes.
My tickets are floating in the bath

tub full of water. I dry them.
One cat is in my purse
but my wallet has dissolved.
The tickets are still dripping.

I look at the clock as it leaps
forward and see I have missed
my plane. My bed is gone now.
There is one cat the size of a sofa.

Kamasutra for dummies

Years ago I had a lover who got bored.
He liked a challenge. I was
too easily pleased to fluff his ego.
He bought a manual. We would
work our way through the positions.

Work is the operant word. I remember
his horny toenails and ripe feet
either side of my eyes and cheeks.
I remember arching my back
like a cat, the ache just looming.

In some positions his prick slipped
out every other stroke and he would
curse. It was sensual as those videos
to flatten your abs or firm your buttocks
where three young women whose abs

are flat as floorboards grin like rigor
mortis as they demonstrate some
overpriced 800 number device.
They never sweat. But we did.
We used chairs. And tables and stools.

Always the manual was open beside us
guiding our calisthenics. Spontaneous
as a concession speech, exciting
as a lecture on actuarial tables
he staked my quivering libido through

its smoking heart. The night he wanted
to try it standing with me upsidedown
I left him hanging from the door
and whoosh, zoomed off like a rabid bat
to find someone who actually liked sex.

The first time I tasted you

The first time I tasted you I thought
strange: metallic, musty, with salt
and cinnamon, the sea
and the kitchen
safety and danger.

The second time I tasted you I thought
known: already known,
perhaps in an oasis of dream
in the desert of a hard night
the dry wind parching me.

I tasted the fruit of a tree
that promised not life
but love, the knowledge
of being known at last
down to my gnarly pit.

What we know and don't
of each other goes on
a voyage not infinite
but long enough, notching
years on our bones.

From your body I eat
and drink all I will ever
know of passionate love
from now till death
drains the chalice.

Colors passing through us

Purple as tulips in May, mauve
into lush velvet, purple
as the stain blackberries leave
on the lips, on the hands,
the purple of ripe grapes
sunlit and warm as flesh.

Every day I will give you a color,
like a new flower in a bud vase
on your desk. Every day
I will paint you, as women
color each other with henna
on hands and on feet.

Red as henna, as cinnamon,
as coals after the fire is banked,
the cardinal in the feeder,
the roses tumbling on the arbor
their weight bending the wood
the red of the syrup I make from their petals.

Orange as the perfumed fruit
hanging their globes on the glossy tree,
orange as pumpkins in the field,
orange as butterflyweed and the monarchs
who come to eat it, orange as my
cat running lithe through the high grass.

Yellow as a goat's wise and wicked eyes,
yellow as a hill of daffodils,
yellow as dandelions by the highway,
yellow as butter and egg yolks,
yellow as a school bus stopping you,
yellow as a slicker in a downpour.

Here is my bouquet, here is a sing
song of all the things you make
praise for the height and depth
of you and the width too.
Here is my box of new crayons at your feet.

Green as mint jelly, green
as a frog on a lily pad twanging,
the green of cos lettuce upright
about to bolt into opulent towers,
green as Grande Chartreuse in a clear
glass, green as wine bottles.

Blue as cornflowers, delphiniums,
bachelor's buttons. Blue as Roquefort,
blue as Saga. Blue as still water.
Blue as the eyes of a Siamese cat.
Blue as shadows on new snow, as a spring
azure sipping from a puddle on the blacktop.

Cobalt as the midnight sky
when day has gone without a trace
and we lie in each other's arms
eyes shut and fingers open
and all the colors of the world
pass through our bodies like strings of fire.

from
The Crooked Inheritance

Tracks

The small birds leave cuneiform
messages on the snow: *I have*
been here, I am hungry, I
must eat. Where I dropped
seeds they scrape down
to pine needles and frozen sand.

Sometimes when snow flickers
past the windows, muffles trees
and bushes, buries the path,
the jays come knocking with their beaks
on my bedroom window:
to them I am made of seeds.

To the cats, I am mother and lover,
lap and toy, cook and cleaner.
To the coyotes I am chaser and shouter.
To the crows, watcher, protector.
To the possums, the foxes, the skunks:
a shadow passing, a moment's wind.

I was bad watchful mommy to one man.
To another I was forgiving sister
whose hand poured out honey and aloe;
to that woman I was a gale whose lashing
waves threatened her foundation; to this
one, an oak to her flowering vine.

I have worn the faces, the masks
of hieroglyphs, gods and demons,
bat faced ghosts, sibyls and thieves,
lover, loser, red rose and ragweed,
these are the tracks I have left
on the white crust of time.

The crooked inheritance

A short neck like my mother
long legs like my father
my grandmother's cataract of hair
and my grandmother's cataracts
my father's glaucoma
my mother's stout heart
my father's quick temper
my mother's curiosity
my father's rationality
my mother's fulsome breasts
my father's narrow feet

Yet only my grandmother saw in me
a remembrance of children past
You have a good quick mind like Moishe.
Your grandfather zecher l'vrocho
had a gift for languages too.
Rivka also had weak eyes
and a delicate stomach.
You can run as fast as Feygeleh.
You know that means little bird?

I was a nest of fledglings chirping
hunger and a future of flight
to her, but to my parents,
the misshapen duckling
who failed to make flesh
their dreams of belonging:
a miraculous blond angel
who would do everything
right they had failed.
Instead they got a black
haired poet who ran away.

Talking with my mother

"I don't believe in heaven or any of that
horseshit tied up with bows," she says.
"That's one advantage being Jewish
among all the troubles I had: you don't
have to buy that nonsense. I'm just dead."

"Okay," I say, "but just suppose. Of your
three husbands, who would you want
waiting on the other side? Would they
line up? Would you have all three?"
"None," she says, "to hell with them.

I always remember the one I didn't
go off with. That's the one I would
think of when I lay awake beside
their snores. But likely he'd have turned
out the same. Piggy, cold, jealous,

self-occupied. Now that I'm dead
I don't have to worry I have no skills,
only worked as a chambermaid.
I'll live by myself in a clean house
with a cat or maybe two. Males.

Females are sluts. Like you," she
says, pointing. "I'll cook what I
like for a change—do the dead eat?"
"How would I know?" I ask. "Well,"
she says, "you're writing the dialogue.

I liked your poems, but the novels—
too much sex. In your books too
much, in my last thirty years,
too little. Remember," she says, "you
never stop wanting it till you're dead.

No, I think I'll stay quiet. No more
money troubles, no more too fat,
too thin, no more of his contempt
and his sly relatives picking at me.
Let me go down into dirt and sleep."

Swear it

My mother swore ripely, inventively
a flashing storm of American and Yiddish
thundering onto my head and shoulders.
My father swore briefly, like an ax
descending on the nape of a sinner.

But all the relatives on my father's
side, *gosh,* they said, *goldarnit.*
What happened to those purveyors
of soft putty cussing, *go to heck,*
they would mutter, *you son of a gun.*

They had limbs instead of legs.
Privates encompassed everything
from bow to stern. They did
number one and number two
and eventually, perhaps, *it.*

It has always amazed me there are
words too potent to say to those
whose ears are tender as baby
lettuces—often those who label
us into narrow jars with salt and

vinegar, saying, *People like them,*
meaning me and mine. Never say
the k or n word, just quietly shut
and bolt the door. Just politely
insert your foot in the Other's face.

Motown, Arsenal of Democracy

Fog used to bloom off the distant river
turning our streets strange, elongating
sounds and muffling others. The crack
of a gunshot softened.

The sky at night was a dull red:
a bonfire built of old creosote soaked
logs by the railroad tracks. A red
almost pink painted by factories—

that never stopped their roar
like traffic in canyons of New York.
But stop they did and fell down
ending dangerous jobs that paid.

We believed in our unions like some
trust in their priests. We believed
in Friday paychecks sure as
winter's ice curb to curb

where older boys could play
hockey dodging cars—wooden
pucks, sticks cracking wood
on wood. A man came home

with a new car and other men
would collect around it like ants
in sugar. Women clumped for showers—
wedding and baby—wakes, funerals

care for the man brought home
with a hole ripped in him, children

coughing. We all coughed in Detroit.
We woke at dawn to my father's hack.

That world is gone as a tableau
of wagon trains. Expressways carved
neighborhoods to shreds. Rich men
moved jobs south, then overseas.

Only the old anger lives there
bubbling up like chemicals dumped
seething now into the water
building now into the bones.

Tanks in the streets

Tanks that year roared through
streets lined with bosomy elms—
tanks with slowly turning turrets
like huge dinosaur heads
their slitted gaze staring us down,
soldiers with rifles cradled
in their arms like babies
stalking past the corner drugstore.

They were entering a foreign land
occupied by dangerous natives:
Detroit: a pool of rainbow
slithering oil ringed by suburbs
of brick colonials and ranches,
then the vast half hidden
fortified houses of those who
grew rich off Detroit.

Class hatred was ground into
my palms like grease into
my brother's hands, like coal
dust into my uncle's. TV
had not yet taught us we
were nothing and only
celebrities had lives that
counted. We poured into

the streets, but the ones we
struck with our rocks, bottles
were each other, white against
Black, Polack against Jew,
Irish against hillbilly. Always,
after the tanks rolled off
it was our corpses strewn
in every riot, in every war.

The Hollywood haircut

I pay $40 to have my haircut.
Last night I saw on television
from Hollywood a $400 haircut.

If I had a $400 haircut
would traffic part for me on the highway
like the Red Sea?

Would men one third my age
follow me panting in the street
and old men faint as I passed?

If I had a $400 haircut
would my books become best
sellers and all my bills be written paid?

If I had a $400 haircut
would I have more orgasms
louder ones; would my eyelashes curl?

If I had a $400 haircut
would people buy calendars
just me on every month grinning?

If I had a $400 haircut
would everyone love me and
would you volunteer

to come clean my house
iron my never ironed shirts
and weed my jungle garden?

No? I thought so.
I'll stick to Sarah
and my $40 trim.

The good, the bad and the inconvenient

Gardening is often a measured cruelty:
what is to live and what is to be torn
up by its roots and flung on the compost
to rot and give its essence to new soil.

It is not only the weeds I seize.
I go down the row of new spinach
their little bright Vs crowding
and snatch every other, flinging

their little bodies just as healthy,
just as sound as their neighbors
but judged, by me, superfluous.
We all commit crimes too small

for us to measure, the ant soldiers
we stomp, whose only aim was to
protect, to feed their vast family.
It is I who decide which beetles

are "good" and which are "bad"
as if each is not whole in its kind.
We eat to live and so do they,
the locusts, the grasshoppers,

flea beetles, aphids and slugs.
By bad I mean inconvenient. Nothing
we do is simple, without consequence
and each act is shadowed with death.

Intense

One morning they are there:
silken nets where the sun ignites
water drops to sparks of light—
handkerchiefs of bleached chiffon
spread over the grasses, stretched
among kinickkinick and heather.

Spiders weave them all at once
hatched and ready, brief splendor.
Walking to pick beans, I tear them.
I can't avoid their evanescent glitter.

I have never seen the little spinners
who make of my ragged lawn and meadow
an encampment of white tents
as if an army of tiny seraphim had deployed—
how beautiful are your tents O Israel—
the hand- or leggywork of hungry spiders
extruding a tent city from swollen bellies.

How to make pesto

Go out in mid sunny morning
a day bright as a bluejay's back
after the dew has vanished
fading like the memory of a dream.

Go with scissors and basket.
Snip to encourage branching.
Never strip the basil plant
but fill the basket to overarching.

Take the biggest garlic cloves
and cut them in quarters to ease
off the paper that hides the ivory
tusk within. Grind Parmesan.

I use pine nuts. Olive oil
must be a virgin. I like Greek
or Sicilian. Now the aroma
fills first the nose, then the kitchen.

The UPS man in the street sniffs.
The neighbors complain; the cats
don't. We eat it on pasta, chicken,
on lamb, on beans, on salmon

and zucchini. We add it to salad
dressings. We rub it behind our
ears. We climb into a tub of pesto
giggling to make aromatic love.

The moon as cat as peach

The moon is a white cat in a peach tree.
She is licking her silky fur
making herself perfect.

This is only a moment
round as a peach you have
not yet bitten into.

If you do not eat it,
it will rot. The peach
offers itself like a smile.

It cares only for the pit
hiding within. The cat
is waiting for prey.

She is indifferent
to the noisy boasting sun
that rattles like a truck

up the dawn sky clanging.
It is too early for such
clatter. She curls into sleep.

Tomorrow she will begin to hide
until you cannot see her
at all. She smiles.

August like lint in the lungs

If Jell-O could be hot, it would be this air.
Needles under the pines are bleached
to straw but mushrooms poke up white
yellow, red—wee beach umbrellas of poison.

Everything sags—oak leaf, tomato
plant, spiky candelabra of lilies,
papers, me. Sun burns acetylene.
Shade's a cave where dark waters bless.

Then up the radar of the weather channel
a red wave seeps toward us. Limp air
stiffens. Wind rushes over the house
tearing off leaves as the sky curdles.

The cat hides under the bed. We slam
windows and the door slams itself.
Everything is swirling as the army
of the rain advances toward us

flattening the tall grasses. Waves
break their knuckles on the roof.
Missiles of water pock the glass.
We feel under water and siege.

Then the rain stops suddenly
as if a great switch had been thrown.
Even the trees look dazed. Heat
creeps back in like a guilty dog.

Metamorphosis

On the folds of the cocoon
segmented, coiled
like a little brown stairway
his fingers are gentle.

In the next chamber
he coaxes a newly hatched
green and purple caterpillar
onto a leaf, stroking it.

We all care for something,
someone. Maybe just our-
selves or family or money.
He loves butterflies.

He built a museum to them,
a sanctuary of fluttering.
Blue morphos, owl
eyes, cattle pinks, orange

and red and black,
umber, lemon, speckled
and zebra striped
they zigzag round us.

Cold leans against the windows.
The roads are clogged
with ice, walled with old
grey snow like cement.

Here the air is warm
moist in our nostrils.
Flowers thicken it.
Now he is placing a cocoon

in a glass container
to change itself, hidden—
as if in a mummy case
an angel should form.

It will be a tobacco hornworm
moth, he says. We pick
them off our tomato plants
Woody says, proud that we

never spray. The custodian
is shocked. You can buy
tomatoes at the super-
market, he says.

Not like ours, I say. A seed
the size of a freckle
turning into a five foot
vine bearing red globes

big as my fist with
the true taste of summer
is miracle too: my garden's
yearly metamorphosis.

Choose a color

Between red and dead, we lived frightened
crouching, covering, signing loyalty oaths.
The war they called cold froze our brains.
The Russians were coming to burn
our flags and steal our color TVs.

Between green and machine, the ozone
fades away scorching our flesh. Glaciers
seep into the sea. Hurricanes come
in quick posses. Drought or torrent.
Polar bears drown swimming for land.

Between blue and Prozac, who will
you be? The brooks are grey with
antibiotics, antidepressants, pain
killers. The fish sleep upsidedown.
This pill will make you inane.

Between lavender and hellfire,
preachers froth. Get saved again,
again. Yet it still itches. In the
dark, what you really want licks
your thighs, burns hot in your brain.

Between white and night, dark
faces invade your entitlement.
They are stealing your birthright
to stomp and swell. Why can't
the world be peopled by only you?

Pick a color, any color from zero
to infinity, from blood to cancer,
from war to Armageddon, from AIDS
to bone, from here to no one
on a very fast jet.

Deadlocked wedlock

Marriage is one man and one woman
they say, one at a time, then another, another.
You see the buffed faces of old men shining
with money as they lead their young blonds
and toddlers, second or third families,
the shopworn wives donated to Goodwill.

It has always been so, they say,
one man and one woman in the Bible—
like Jacob with Leah and Rachel
and two bondmaidens dropping children,
his four women competing to swell
like a galaxy of moons.

In Tibet women had various husbands at once.
I had two myself for a few years.
In earlier times and different cultures
and tribes, men married men and women
married women, and the sky never fell.
People loved as they would and must

and the rivers still ran clean and the grass
grew a lot thicker and more abundantly
than it does with us. What damage
does love do in the soft grey evenings
when the rain drifts like pigeon feathers
across the sky and into the trees?

Why, gentlemen, do you fear two women
who walk holding hands with their child?
Two fifty-year-old men exchange rings
and kiss, and you catch mad cow disease?
What do you hate when you watch
lovers? What are you really missing?

Money is one of those things

Money is one of those things like health:
when you have it you feel entitled.
It's part of you like your left elbow
or your front teeth. But they can

easily be pulled and so can your
credit, your wage, all that money
you squirreled away in stocks
going up like rockets on the 4th.

Money never belongs to us.
It's a paper fiction we believe
like the first guy who says
in the backseat he loves you.

He's already planning a move
on a cheerleader, but his voice trembles
a little and you're too young to
know it's his hardon talking.

Money comes on that way. You
want that, it tells you, you got to have
a new couch, a new car, a new nose.
I'll make you so happy, it croons,

I'll make you shine like a gas fire
burning in a car that just rearended
an SUV, and don't you want one too?
I love you, I'm yours forever

money sings, you're so important,
unique, I'm your love slave.
Just make a central place for me
in your heart, your hearth. Right

there where your brain used to be.
Oh, it comes and it goes like a tide
pulled by a titanium moon, and what
it truly loves and obeys is power.

In our name

In your name, we have invaded
come with planes, tanks and artillery
into a country and wonder why
they do not like us
be proud

In your name we have bombed villages
and towns and left torn babies
the bloated bellies of their mothers
a little boy crying for his father
who lies under his broken house
the smashed arms of teenagers
in the sunbaked streets
every death creates a warrior
be proud

In our name we have taken men
and women from their homes
in the afternoon breaking down their doors
in the night waking them to the rattle
of weapons leaving their children
weeping with fear
be proud

In your name we have taken those we suspect
because they were in the wrong place
or because someone who hated them gave their name
or because a soldier didn't like the way they stared at him
put them in cells and strung them up like slaughtered cattle
stripped their clothes and mocked them naked
ran electricity through their tender parts

set dogs to rip their flesh
in your name
be proud

This is who we are becoming.
There is none other but us sanctioning this.
In our name young boys from Newark and Sandusky
are shot at by people who live in the place
they have been marched to.
in our name a young woman from Detroit
is disemboweled by a bomb.
In our name the sons of out of work miners
step on land mines.
In our name their bodies are shipped home.
In our name fathers return to their children
maimed and blind, their brains sered.

This is who we are in Athens or in Lima not Ohio
when people glare at us in the street.
This is the person my passport identifies,
the one who allows the order to be given
for blood to be mixed with sand
for bones to be mixed with mud

In our name is all this being carried out right now
as we sit here, as we speak, as we sleep.
Every day we do not act, we are permitting.
Every day we do not say no, we all say yes
be proud.

Bashert*

Remember when you invited me into
your kitchen and cut a ripe mango:
orange, deep scented, juicy on a green
platter. I thought then, perhaps
we will be lovers.

Remember when you came up the gravel
drive and I fed you my grandmother's
sour cherry soup, cold and touched
with cream. You wondered
then, could we be lovers?

So many years worn away, smoothed
in the swift waters of memory.
Suppose you had not driven out
that June day, suppose it had rained
suppose I had accepted a former

lover's Iowa invitation. Suppose,
a hundred forking divergent moments
like the intricate web of a cracked
pond ice. Or maybe the dividing
paths of a myriad other choices

would have joined back to the master
trunk where we clasp each other
murmuring love. I was the juicy
mango you bit into that day, and you
are my sweet and my sour

my past and my future, my best
hope and my worst fear, my friend
and brother and sparring partner.
Chance or fate, we grasped what
was offered us and we hold on.

*the destined one

The lived in look

My second mother-in-law had white carpeting
white sofa with blue designer touches.
Everything sparkled. Walking on the beach
I got tar on bare feet. Footprints

across that arctic expanse marred
perfection. I have never eaten
without dribbles and droplets exploding
from me like wet sparks on tablecloth

on my clothes, on the ceiling,
miraculously appearing five blocks
away as stigmata on statues. In short
a certain limited chaos exudes from

my pores. Everyone over fifty was born
to a world where ideal housewives
scrubbed floors to blinding gloss
in pearls and taffeta dresses on TV.

Women came with umbilical cords
leading to vacuum cleaners. You
plugged in a wife and she began
a wash cycle while her eyes spun.

Every three weeks we shovel out
the kitchen and bath. Spanish moss
of webs festoon our rafters. Cat hair
is the decorating theme of our couches.

Don't apologize for walls children
drew robots on, don't blush for last
month's newspapers on the coffee
table under cartons from Sunday's takeout.

This is the sweet imprint of your life
and loves upon the rumpled sheets
of your days. Relax. Breathe deeply.
Mess will make us free.

Mated

You are shoveling snow in the long drive
down to the road, tossing it. From
my window you resemble a great
downcoated bear shaking himself dry.

You cannot make a good omelet;
I cannot fence the tomato garden.
You cannot balance a checkbook;
I cannot pull out a rusted screw.

I can make perfect pie dough; you
can plow all the gardens by dusk.
I can speak French and Spanish,
learn languages enough to manage

Czech, Greek, Norwegian, what
ever travel requires; you can drive
on the wrong side of roads, conquer
roundabouts an hour out of Heathrow.

I can read maps; you read spread-
sheets, wiring diagrams. That's
what mating is, the inserting of
parts that together make completion

prick and cunt, word and answer
all the antiphony of love.

My grandmother's song

We were girls, said my grandmother.
We went to the river with our laundry
to beat it on the stones, washing
it clean, and then we spread it
on the wide grey boulders to dry.

We were laughing, said my grandmother
all of us girls together unmarried
and mostly unafraid, although of course
as Jews we were always a little on edge.
You know how a sparrow pecks seeds

always watching, listening for danger
to pounce. We gossiped about bad
girls over the river and boys and who
had peeked at us as we passed.
We took off our clothes, hung them

on bushes and bathed in the cool
rushing water, talking of Maidele
who threw herself in the current
to carry her big belly away, telling
of ghosts and dybbuks, of promises.

Then grandmother would sigh and dab
a small tear, and I would wonder
what she missed. I would rather
bathe in a tub, I said, in warm water.
The mikvah was warm, she said, and

the river was cold, but we liked
the river, young girls who did not
guess what would happen to us, how
our hopes would melt like candle wax
how we would bear and bear children

like apples falling from the tree
so many, but a tree that bled
and some would just rot in the grass.
You never forget the ones who die
she said even if you only held them

two months or twelve, they come
back in the night and circle like fish
opening silent mouths and never
do they grow older, but you do.
Your hair hangs like strands

of a worn-out mop, your flesh
puffs up like bread from too much yeast
or dwindles till your arms are brittle
sticks and the frost never leaves you.
I want to go down to the river

again, I want to hear the singing
and tell stories with friends we would
never tell in front of our mothers.
I want to go down to the river,
wade in and let it wash my bones

down to the hope that must surely
still form their marrow, deep
and rich in spite of the sights
that have dimmed my eyes
and tears that have pickled my heart.

The birthday of the world

On the birthday of the world
I begin to contemplate
what I have done and left
undone, but this year
not so much rebuilding

of my perennially damaged
psyche, shoring up eroding
friendships, digging out
stumps of old resentments
that refuse to rot on their own.

No, this year I want to call
myself to task for what
I have done and not done
for peace. How much have
I dared in opposition?

How much have I put
on the line for freedom?
For mine and others?
As these freedoms are pared,
sliced and diced, where

have I spoken out? Who
have I tried to move? In
this holy season, I stand
self-convicted of sloth
in a time when lies choke

the mind and rhetoric
bends reason to slithering
choking pythons. Here
I stand before the gates
opening, the fire dazzling

my eyes and as I approach
what judges me, I judge
myself. Give me weapons
of minute destruction. Let
my words turn into sparks.

N'eilah

The hinge of the year:
the great gates opening
and then slowly slowly
closing on us.

I always imagine those gates
hanging over the ocean
fiery over the stone grey
waters of evening.

We cast what we must
change about ourselves
onto the waters flowing
to the sea. The sins,

errors, bad habits, whatever
you call them, dissolve.
When I was little I cried
out I! I! I! I want I want.

Older, I feel less important,
a worker bee in the hive
of history, miles of hard
labor to make my sweetness.

The gates are closing
The light is failing
I kneel before what I love
imploring that it may live.

So much breaks, wears
down, fails in us. We must
forgive our broken promises—
their sharp shards in our hands.

In the sukkah

Open to the sky
as our lives truly are
for down upon us can rain
all that our world has to offer—
sun and sleet, bombs and debris,

bits of space junk, meteorites
the red and yellow leaves
just beginning to color
and drift like open wings
of butterflies spiraling down—

we sit in our makeshift hut
willfully transitory, dressed
with the fruit of harvest
pumpkins, apples and nuts.
This is the feast where we

are commanded to be glad,
to rejoice in the bounty of earth
fat or meager. We're exposed.
Seldom do we sit or sleep
outside in this cooling time

as the earth plunges
toward darkness and ice.
We hear owls, the surviving
crickets, the rustling of fast
small life in the underbrush,

the padding of raccoons,
coywolves howling at the full moon
from down in the marsh.
It is a kind of nakedness
to strip off our houses

like snails left unprotected
and let the stars poke
into our skulls till we seem
to fall upward. How intimate
we are now with the night.

The full moon of Nisan

The full moon of Nisan pulls us
almost every Jew under the sky
to a table. Like a tide composed
of tiny rivulets we head
purposefully toward our seders
laden with the flat tasteless
bread of haste.

The moon when it rises looks
like strawberry ice cream.
Then it lightens to waxy cheese.
Then it soars pale and pitted
like matzoh, the old kind
round instead of square
dry and winking.

Nisan brings the matzoh moon
urging buds to open, urging
minds to fling their gates
wide on the night we become
slaves and then march out
to freedom past lintels
smeared with blood.

Peace in a time of war

A puddle of amber light
like sun spread on a table,
food flirting savor into the nose,
faces of friends, a vase
of daffodils and Dutch iris:

this is an evening of honey
on the tongue, cinnamon
scented, red wine sweet
and dry, voices rising
like a flock of swallows

turning together in evening
air. Darkness walls off
the room from what lies
outside, the fire and dust
and blood of war, bodies

stacked like firewood
burst like overripe melons.
Ceremony is a moat we have
crossed into a moment's
harmony, as if the world paused—

but it doesn't. What we must
do waits like coats tossed
on the bed, for us to rise
from this warm table
put on again and go out.

The cup of Eliyahu

In life you had a temper.
Your sarcasm was a whetted knife.
Sometimes you shuddered with fear
but you made yourself act no matter
how few stood with you.
Open the door for Eliyahu
that he may come in.

Now you return to us
in rough times, out of smoke
and dust that swirls blinding us.
You come in vision, you come
in lightning on blackness.
Open the door for Eliyahu
that he may come in.

In every generation you return
speaking what few want to hear
words that burn us, that cut
us loose so we rise and go again
over the sharp rocks upward.
Open the door for Eliyahu
that he may come in.

You come as a wild man,
as a homeless sidewalk orator,
you come as a woman taking the bima,
you come in prayer and song,

you come in a fierce rant.
Open the door for Eliyahu
that she may come in.

Prophecy is not a gift, but
sometimes a curse, Jonah
refusing. It is dangerous
to be right, to be righteous.
To stand against the wall of might.
Open the door for Eliyahu
that he may come in.

There are moments for each
of us when you summon, when
you call the whirlwind, when you
shake us like a rattle: Then we
too must become you and rise.
Open the door for Eliyahu
that we may come in.

The wind of saying

The words dance in the wind of saying.
They are leaves that crispen,
sere, turning to dust. As long
as that language runs its blood-

rich river through the tongues
of people, as long as grand
mothers weave the warp and woof
of old stories with bright new

words carpeting the air
into dreams, then the words
live like good bacteria
within our guts, feeding us.

We catch the letters and trap
them in books, pearlescent butterflies
pinned down. We fasten the letters
with nails to the white pages.

Most words dry finally to husks
even though dead languages
whisper, blown sand through
the dim corridors of library stacks.

Languages wither, languages
are arrested and die in prison,
stories are chopped off at the roots
like weeds, lullabies spill

on the floor and dry up.
Conquerors force their words
into the minds of their victims.
Our natural language is a scream.

Our natural language is a cry
rattling in the night. But tongues
are how we touch, how we reach,
how we teach, the spine of words.

Some New Poems

The low road

What can they do
to you? Whatever they want.
They can set you up, they can
bust you, they can break
your fingers, they can
burn your brain with electricity,
blur you with drugs till you
can't walk, can't remember, they can
take your child, wall up
your lover. They can do anything
you can't stop them
from doing. How can you stop
them? Alone, you can fight,
you can refuse, you can
take what revenge you can
but they roll over you.

Two people can keep each other
sane, can give support, conviction,
love, massage, hope, sex.
Three people are a delegation,
a committee, a wedge. With four
you can play bridge and start
an organization. With six
you can rent a whole house,
eat pie for dinner with no

seconds and hold a fund-raising party.
A dozen make a demonstration.
A hundred fill a hall.

A thousand have solidarity and your own newsletter;
ten thousand, power and your own paper;
a hundred thousand, your own media;
ten million, your own country.

It goes on one at a time,
it starts when you care
to act, it starts when you do
it again after they said *No,*
it starts when you say *We*
and know who you mean, and each
day you mean one more.

The curse of Wonder Woman

Batman can suffer angst in his batcave,
pester his butler factotum with doubts,
question his adoption of Robin,
but Wonder Woman can never waver.

She must fight, fight, fight without
recompense. No 3 a.m. nitpicking
of a festering conscience for her.
Role models can't stop to consider.

Role models can't whine or take
to their beds with PMS or enjoy
a headache with chocolates
on the couch. Women are watching,

judging, waiting for the cracks
in the makeup to show. Role
models can't enjoy a fling in Jamaica.
They don't get vacations or spas.

People need and resent role models
with equal fervor. She'd like to
retire, but who else can bounce
back bullets on a quest for justice?

She's stuck in the spotlight impaled
by duty. Sometimes she half wishes
to fail and be replaced by some other
woman without sense to be afraid.

July Sunday 10 a.m.

We drink café au lait on the sunporch,
Puck has dozed off paws in the air
lying on the rumpled morning paper.
Through the screens, a scent of roses
and the repeated cry of a cardinal
shaped like a sickle. You wear only
red silk boxers. I wear my thinnest
nightgown. The air is heavy
with pollen and the sun sparkles
on the rhododendrons as if they
had just been waxed.

Football for dummies

Among my husbands and lovers,
I had never before lived
with a sports fan. Hockey
he does not follow, but base-
ball, basketball, football all
in their seasons consume him.
I had to share something:

baseball is too slow. Basket-
ball goes on for months
and months, interminably,
a herd of skinny giants
running back and forth mys-
terious as a flock of swallows
wheeling together at twilight.

But football: it's only sixteen
Sundays and maybe playoffs.
That seemed reasonable. I
bought a book. Now every
Sunday in season I stare
avidly while huge millionaires
collide like rival rhinoceros.

When we watch the Super
Bowl with groups of men
and I explain a nickel
back they gaze at me
with esoteric lust. I
look only at the screen.
Football, it is mine.

Murder, unincorporated

I am of the opinion that almost
anyone would kill for something—
an idea, a country on a map or
in the head, a god or goddess,
a lover, a child, a hovel, a home.

A stash of money or drugs,
a meal, a blanket, medicine,
personal morality as in kill
the bitch, a real Picasso
a mother, a father, prized

stallion, prize bull, a dog.
To stay out of prison, to cross
a border to safety, to cover
up a lie, a theft, to maintain
cover, to steal identity.

Because the gun was in
the drawer, the ax on the
table, the chance lay open
like a switchblade and temper
sparked a blaze only blood

could cool. Because
the sergeant said to.
Because the others did.

The happy man

Pierre-Joseph Redouté painted roses;
also succulents, lilies, rare tropical
imports, but most famously, roses.

He was from a family of journeymen
painters, never famous, portraits
to order, flattering of course,

church and abbey decorations.
But Redouté painted flowers. He
looked like a peasant, squarish

in body, strong with huge mishapen
hands, not what aristocrats or critics
expect. But Redouté painted flowers.

He ambled through courts, Marie
Antoinette's play village at Versailles,
Revolution, Terror, Napoléon. Josephine's

triumph and her divorce, Charles X,
Louis-Philippe, court painter to each
in turn unfailingly friendly, painting flowers.

His younger brother drew beetles
and reptiles instead of court ladies
or kings, but Redouté painted flowers.

Money came to him like rain to a garden.
He drank it in blindly, gave it to others,
spent it like the water it seemed.

Always more tomorrow. He grew old,
unfashionable. Moneylenders sucked
him dry but he never drooped. Flowers

were always calling. At the end poor
but busy, brush in hand he died smiling
as he painted a perfect white lily.

Collectors

Some people collect grudges
like stamps or rare coins.
They take out their prize holdings
to polish till they glow.

But after a while, it doesn't work
any longer, so they need fresh
ones to cherish the way another
will groom a champion setter.

Friendships are expendable
as last decade's palazzo pants.
Rejecting is more fun than
holding close. So on they go

their paths littered with torn
and discarded friendships,
like bones outside the den
of a fairy tale giant.

First sown

Peas are the first thing we plant
always. We lie full length
on the cold black earth and poke
holes in it for the wrinkled
old men of the seeds.

Nothing will happen for weeks.
Rain will soak them, a white
tablecloth of snow will cover
them and be whisked off.
The moon will sing to them:

open, loosen, let the pale
shoots break out. No,
they are pebbles, they sit
in the earth like false teeth.
They ignore the sweet sun.

Then one unlikely day
the soil cracks along miniature
faults and soon baby leaves
stick out their double heads
and we know we shall have peas.

Away with all that

Where the Herring River meets Wellfleet Bay
the tide carries brackish water out to sea.
I arrive with my pants pocket stuffed
with stale bread. As I tear off each piece
I name what I am praying will depart.

Envy and prejudice sink under their own
weight like hunks of granite. Impatience
darts out into the bay waters, vanishing
as a fish rises to gulp it. Procrastination,
sloth eddy back and forth at waves' edge.

Conceit prances out on wave tops.
Anger and malice bounce off each other
and sink down onto the sand. Intention
never carried out simply comes apart.
It is all me. It is all I wish were not me.

Wishing won't do it any more than old
bread can rid me of what I must pry
out of myself every day, intention
that wears through like an old runner
on stairs I must climb to the top.

If only I could discard my rotten parts
as simply as I toss these bits of bread
too hard to eat onto waves that push,
push, push my named sins to the bay,
to bigger bay, out into the world ocean.

All that remains

A pillar of salt would slowly dissolve
in the season of rains, as women
have so often melted from history
so many nameless, wife of,
daughter of, maidservant of.

Their faces peer out between
the black logs and squiggles
of Hebrew letters, as if through
bars. We were here too, they
whisper like pages turning,

pages on which their fates
are sometimes written, always
by others. The strongest ones,
Miriam, Deborah, hold their
names gripped in their teeth.

Diving through the letters
into the white light between
I seek them out, wife of,
daughter of, maidservant of—
their silence deafens me.

What comes next

After a hurricane the whine
of chainsaws cutting into downed trees.

After a blizzard, whiteout silence
then the cries of hungry birds.

After a loss, another kind
of silence when we are too weary

to cry, too numb to tackle
the list of things that must be done.

The force of what has happened
flattens us to old rugs

on which the pattern is only
memory and their use is past.

Where dreams come from

A girl slams the door of her little room
under the eaves where marauding squirrels
scamper overhead like herds of ideas.
She has forgotten to be grateful she has
finally a room with a door that shuts.

She is furious her parents don't comprehend
why she wants to go to college, that place
of musical comedy fantasies and weekend
football her father watches, beer can
in hand. It is as if she announced I want

to journey to Iceland or Machu Picchu.
Nobody in their family goes to college.
Where do dreams come from? Do they
sneak in through torn screens at night
to light on the arm like mosquitoes?

Are they passed from mouth to ear
like gossip or dirty jokes? Do they
sprout from underground on damp
mornings like toadstools that form
fairy rings on dewtipped grasses?

No, they slink out of books, they lurk
in the stacks of libraries. Out of pages
turned they rise like the scent of peonies
and infect the brain with their promise.
I want, I will, says the girl and already

she is halfway out the door and down
the street from this neighborhood, this
mortgaged house, this family tight
and constricting as the collar on the next
door dog who howls on his chain all night.

The tao of touch

What magic does touch create
that we crave it so. That babies
do not thrive without it. That
the nurse who cuts tough nails
and sands calluses on the elderly
tells me sometimes men weep
as she rubs lotion on their feet.

Yet the touch of a stranger
the bumping or predatory thrust
in the subway is like a slap.
We long for the familiar, the open
palm of love, its tender fingers.
It is our hands that tamed cats
into pets, not our food.

The widow looks in the mirror
thinking, no one will ever touch
me again, never. Not hold me.
Not caress the softness of my
breasts, my inner thighs, the swell
of my belly. Do I still live
if no one knows my body?

We touch each other so many
ways, in curiosity, in anger,
to command attention, to soothe,
to quiet, to rouse, to cure.
Touch is our first language
and often, our last as the breath
ebbs and a hand closes our eyes.

End of days

Almost always with cats, the end
comes creeping over the two of you—
she stops eating, his back legs
no longer support him, she leans
to your hand and purrs but cannot
rise—sometimes a whimper of pain
although they are stoic. They see
death clearly through hooded eyes.

Then there is the long weepy
trip to the vet, the carrier no
longer necessary, the last time
in your lap. The injection is quick.
Simply they stop breathing
in your arms. You bring them
home to bury in the flower garden,
planting a bush over a deep grave.

That is how I would like to cease,
held in a lover's arms and quickly
fading to black like an old-fashioned
movie embrace. I hate the white
silent scream of hospitals, the whine
of pain like air-conditioning's hum.
I want to click the off switch.
And if I can no longer choose

I want someone who loves me
there, not a doctor with forty patients
and his morality to keep me sort
of, kind of alive or sort of undead.
Why are we more rational and kinder
to our pets than to ourselves or our
parents? Death is not the worst
thing; denying it can be.

DATES OF COMPOSITION

The following is a list of poems in this book and the dates they were written, which, as you can see, often is different from the date of book publication.

from STONE, PAPER, KNIFE   1983

A key to common lethal fungi 1980
The common living dirt 1982
Toad dreams 1981
Down at the bottom of things 1981
A story wet as tears 1979
Absolute zero in the brain 1980
Eating my tail 1979
It breaks 1979
What's that smell in the kitchen? 1980
The weight 1980
Very late July 1980
Mornings in various years 1981
Digging in 1981
The working writer 1980
The back pockets of love 1981
Snow, snow 1982
In which she begs (like everybody else) that love may last 1982
Let us gather at the river 1980
Ashes, ashes, all fall down 1979

from MY MOTHER'S BODY   1985

from AVAILABLE LIGHT   1988

from EARLY GRRRL 1999

from THE ART OF BLESSING THE DAY 1999

from COLORS PASSING THROUGH US 2003

from THE CROOKED INHERITANCE 2006

Some NEW POEMS

Football for dummies 2008
Murder, unincorporated 2008
The happy man 2007
Collectors 2010
First sown 2010
Away with all that 2010
All that remains 2010
What comes next 2010
Where dreams come from 2010
The tao of touch 2009
End of days 2006

A NOTE ABOUT THE AUTHOR

Marge Piercy is the author of eighteen collections of poetry, including *Circles on the Water,* a selection from her early works. Among her more recent volumes: *The Crooked Inheritance; Colors Passing Through Us; The Art of Blessing the Day; What Are Big Girls Made Of?; Mars and Her Children; Available Light; My Mother's Body;* and *Stone, Paper, Knife.* In 1990 her poetry won the Golden Rose, the oldest poetry award in the country. She is also the author of a memoir, *Sleeping with Cats,* and seventeen novels, the most recent being *Sex Wars.* Her fiction and poetry have been translated into nineteen languages. She lives on Cape Cod with her husband, Ira Wood, the novelist and public radio interviewer, with whom she has written a play, a novel and most recently the second edition of *So You Want to Write: How to Master the Craft of Fiction and Personal Narrative.*

Marge Piercy's website address is www.margepiercy.com.
She can also be reached on Facebook.

A NOTE ABOUT THE TYPE

This book is set in the typeface Tibere, designed by the French typographer Albert Boton. Born in 1932, he began his career as a cabinetmaker, but later apprenticed with Adrian Frutiger in graphic design and worked as a type designer for the Deberny & Peignot type foundry in Paris. Boton has produced numerous well-known typefaces including Brasilia, Eras, and Elan. Tibere is a visually engaging face, distinguished by sharp serifs and terminals, and moderately sized apertures.

Composed by Creative Graphics, Inc., Allentown, Pennsylvania

Printed and bound by Berryville Graphics, Berryville, Virginia

Book design by Robert C. Olsson